Cybersecurity for Main Street

Cyber Fit in 21 Days

Ann Westerheim, PhD.

Dedicated to the Ekaru team of technology advisors, current and alumni, and all the wonderful local businesses and partners we've worked with over the years.

TABLE OF CONTENTS - YOUR 21 DAY CHECKLIST

INTRODUCTION

CYBERSECURITY: HOW DID THINGS GET SO CRAZY?

**"I'm no expert, but I think it's
some kind of cyber attack!"**

I n May of 2021, drivers along parts of the East Coast waited hours in line at gas stations to fill up, oftentimes only to learn there was no gas left. During the crisis, over one in twenty gas stations in Virginia were completely out of fuel, American Airlines had to add refueling stops for two of its long-haul flights, and gas prices began to soar. How could this be happening?

The Colonial Pipeline, a 5,500-mile major fuel pipeline in the United States that provides gasoline, diesel, and jet fuel to the East Coast, was the target of a ransomware attack. The hackers encrypted the company's data and demanded a ransom to restore access. As a result of the attack, the Colonial Pipeline was forced to shut down for several days, causing a disruption in fuel supply and leading to panic buying and price spikes at gas stations in parts of the country. Images of long lines at gas stations in impacted regions were reminiscent of the 1970s energy crisis when I remember my father waiting in line for hours to get gas – who would have expected to see that again? The event highlighted the vulnerability of critical infrastructure to cyberattacks and the potential consequences of such attacks.

The Colonial Pipeline ransomware event brought cybersecurity to the forefront of many people's minds, with the FBI investigation and updates from the White House on national news daily during the crisis. However, while this event caught people's attention, cybersecurity is in the news almost every day. The year 2023 is off to a rough start with breaches at LifeLock, T-Mobile, PayPal, Chick-fil-A, Twitter, PayPal, MailChimp, Five Guys, Reddit, GoDaddy, Dish Network, U.S. Marshals Service, and more. Also in January of 2023, Iowa's largest school district cancelled classes for two days after a cyberattack, the city of Oakland declared a local state of emergency in February after a ransomware attack forced all its IT systems offline, and the U.S No Fly List with over 1.5 million records of banned flyers was leaked.

Did you know there are ransomware "gangs" and affiliate systems where criminals can buy nefarious software programs to hijack companies for ransom, and split the profits with the parent organization? You don't even need to know how to code to be a cybercriminal. This is big business. In the crazy world we live in, after a ransomware attack on Canada's largest pediatric medical center in December of 2022, the ransomware group LockBit issued a rare apology and offered to provide software to restore the systems after one of their "partners" violated the rules of service by attacking a healthcare organization. Honor among thieves?

Cybersecurity isn't about just some far away "cyber" world in the "cloud". Real people are impacted in everyday life. People can't buy gas. Kids can't go to school. Hospitals can't take care of sick patients. Hard earned money is stolen.

It may sound hopeless to try to stay safe in this wave of crime, but rest assured there are many things you can do to protect yourself, your family, and your local business online.

Cybersecurity for the 99%

This book is about cybersecurity for the 99%. Are you familiar with terms like these: Privilege Escalation, Lateral Movement, DDoS, SOC, APT, CASB, EDR, IAM, SSO, SIEM? If so, then you're part of the cybersecurity 1%, and this book is not for you.

My goal is to create a community movement that is not afraid of cybersecurity and is empowered to have large-scale impact. There are a lot of simple, smart, and affordable things you can do to stay safer online. Get cyber aware and think before you click!

After working in big tech at Digital Equipment Corporation and Intel building Microprocessors for many years, I started a technology consulting company, Ekaru. Ekaru's mission has been "connecting people with technology" and focusing on the "last mile" of technology. After two decades of work helping thousands of people deploy, manage, and protect their technology, I wrote this book to bring that experience to you in a practical and easy-to-use form – Where does all the technology go? How does Main Street use technology? How can we empower everyone – the 99% - to benefit from technology? In a lot of ways, technology is a great equalizer, and at the same time it's created a digital divide.

Cyber Anxiety

Recent cybersecurity headlines are alarming, and sometimes technology can feel like a house of cards – my Roomba vacuum cleaner might be watching me, my Alexa may be eavesdropping on me, my Nest thermostat may be hacked, my Ring Doorbell might be hacked, my car could be hacked, my bank account could be drained, and the list goes on... The World Economic Forum has released their Global Risks Report for 2023 and "Widespread Cybercrime and cyber insecurity" has now entered the top 10 list both for short and long-term global risks.

Technology Optimism

It's not all gloom and doom, though. I'm a technology optimist and am constantly amazed by what technology enables us to do. Technology enables more connections, leveling the playing field for small businesses and individuals to be seen and make a positive impact. With a rideshare app on my phone I can get a ride anywhere when I need it, track the vehicle's location, and complete the payment online without taking out my wallet. I'm also surrounded by digital signs with up-to-date information like flight departures and arrivals, and menus when I'm at the airport. I can order food from anywhere and get it delivered, I can see who's at my door before I answer it, and I can visit my doctor over the computer. No more long-distance phone charges as I can FaceTime friends and family any time I want.

Growing up as a technology enthusiast in a town where IBM Research is located, I got to see a preview of so many cool technologies - robots, gravitational waves, computers... so exciting. Back then, the idea of a computer in every home sounded like science fiction. Fast forward many years and I have more computing power in the palm of my hand with my iPhone than what NASA used to get people to the moon. I even had fun using ChatGPT, the artificial intelligence chatbot by OpenAI, to help get started filling some blank pages as I was putting this book together. Technology is cool and fun! How does technology enable YOU?

So how did it get so crazy? It's all about money!

Computer viruses and malware (malicious software) have been around a long time. The Creeper program, often regarded as the first virus, was created in 1971 by Bob Thomas of BBN. Creeper was initially designed as a security test to see if a self-replicating program was possible. Creeper did no damage, simply displaying a message "I'M THE CREEPER. CATCH ME IF YOU CAN". It was intended merely as a fun joke and to generate some bragging rights about hacking capabilities.

The introduction of Cryptocurrency changed everything and has turned cybercrime into a very profitable business. Cryptocurrency has enabled cybercriminals to act anonymously, fueling an explosion of cybercrime. Without cryptocurrency, what would you do? Pay the ransomware by mailing a check or paying by credit card? These would be easily traceable.

With cryptocurrency, criminals have found a way to make a LOT of money and they don't even need to know how to write software. The "Ransomware as a Service" business model was developed for criminal purposes to make it even easier for criminals to deploy ransomware attacks with little effort and potentially big payouts. Criminals with little or no technical know-how can now blast out millions of emails to potential victims in just a few mouse clicks.

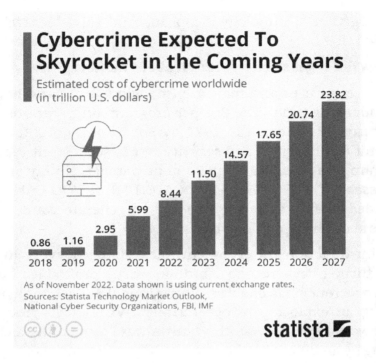

Cybercrime Expected To Skyrocket in the Coming Years

Estimated cost of cybercrime worldwide
(in trillion U.S. dollars)

Year	Value
2018	0.86
2019	1.16
2020	2.95
2021	5.99
2022	8.44
2023	11.50
2024	14.57
2025	17.65
2026	20.74
2027	23.82

As of November 2022. Data shown is using current exchange rates.
Sources: Statista Technology Market Outlook,
National Cyber Security Organizations, FBI, IMF

statista

The financial damages caused by cybercrime continue to grow and are projected to keep growing. Cybercrime is big business! Any business would want to have a growth curve like this. It's not about what your data is worth to criminals, but what is it worth to you?

The Verizon 2022 Data Breach Investigations Report (DBIR) shows that the main motivation for breaches is 96% financial, personal gain, and "fun" (yes that's what some people think about cybercrime), with disagreement, protest, and personal grudge far behind.

The Digital Divide

There's a digital divide here on many levels. Big businesses have more resources and can recover from even a major event, while a small local business with tight margins and limited resources could be wiped out. Target, Marriot, CapitalOne, EquiFax, The Home Depot, Yahoo and other big names have all experienced major cyber incidents, and they've recovered. One in six municipalities has been hit with a cyber incident. Smaller businesses don't make the national headlines when there's a cyber incident, but more than half of incidents hit small businesses. And keep in mind, your data may be leaked in a breach through no fault of your own.

Cybersecurity insights from the Department of Homeland security:

- All businesses, regardless of size, are at risk. Small businesses may feel like they are not targets for cyberattacks either due to their size or the perception that they don't have anything worth stealing.

- Only a small percentage of cyberattacks are considered targeted attacks, meaning the attacker group is going after a particular company or group of companies in order to steal specific data.

- The majority of cyber criminals are indiscriminate; they target vulnerable computer systems regardless of whether the systems are part of a Fortune 500 company, a small business, or belong to a home user.

A positive and optimistic approach to Cybersecurity

Cybersecurity is a big risk, but rest assured there are many smart and affordable thing you can to do stay safer online. There's no scary person in a dark hoodie hunched over a computer in this book. Fear, uncertainty, and doubt (aka "FUD") just trigger a fight, flight, or *freeze* response. Instead, learn about what *you* can do!

Security requires your *participation.*

Here are a few of the concepts we'll cover in this book.

- Don't let fear overwhelm you – there are a lot of smart and affordable things you can do to stay safer online. Take action!

- It's no longer valid to say, "I'm not a tech person". Do you use UBER? Do you bank online? Do you use social media? You're now a tech person, like it or not.
- There's no "silver bullet". No single product or action will keep you secure, and no matter how much you do there's no such thing as 100% secure.
- Convenience vs security – Some of the things that help you stay secure online, like two factor authentication and strong passwords, are inconvenient but are necessary.
- Security is a combination of People, Processes, and Technology.
- While there's always more you can do, anything you do is better than nothing.

Getting Started on a Cyber Fit Journey

What follows is a 21-day guide to getting cyber fit. I'll attempt to explain cybersecurity concepts in plain English (trying not to get too techie), and how they apply to you, your family, and your local business. Read and implement one a day, and you'll be on a path to cyber fitness!

And remember... while knowledge is a critical first step, just like a diet book, if you don't change your behavior, you won't be more secure.

Security requires your participation!

DAY #1 – KEEP YOUR TECHNOLOGY UP TO DATE

© Glasbergen/ glasbergen.com

"It's an internet-ready, tri-mode, LCD color, MP3 compatible, digital wireless communicator. We make them extra big so people will notice how cool you are."

>>OLD technology doesn't protect against NEW threats.

>>**Did you know?** Patch Tuesday is the commonly known name of Microsoft's release of security fixes and occurs the second Tuesday of each month. Patch Tuesday has been around 20 years since October 2003!

New security threats are identified all the time – after all, criminals love to make more money! They look for vulnerabilities and devious ways to exploit them. In this "cat and mouse game", it's important that as new threats are identified, you keep your technology up to date. When you get a notification that "updates are available", don't put it off – do the updates as soon as you can. These are FREE, and worth the inconvenience.

Patch Tuesday

Microsoft is the most popular software provider, running on 1.4 billion computers worldwide. They are very transparent about their updates with their monthly "Patch Tuesday" updates, released on the second Tuesday of the month (in addition to a few "out of band" releases for critical updates). Security vulnerabilities are discovered through research, and then they're patched. If you get the patch, then you're safe for that vulnerability.

We often get questions about why Microsoft seems so unsafe – why do they have so many things to fix each month? While Microsoft is very visible with their updates, ALL technology needs to be kept up to date, not just Microsoft! You know all those "update" announcements you see on your iPhone? Those also include security patches, but Apple isn't as transparent about explaining what they are. Adobe, Android, Cisco, Chrome, Zoom, and all your favorite tech is vulnerable to new security threats and needs to be kept up to date.

Technology Lifecycle

At some point, the technology you own will be retired from support, and you'll need to upgrade to a new version. At that point, they will no longer provide technical support, bug fixes, or security fixes. This includes security updates which can help protect your PC from harmful viruses, spyware, and other malicious software like ransomware.

Microsoft generally supports products for ten years providing updates along the way. As an example, Windows 10 Home and Pro was released July 29, 2015, and will be supported through October 14, 2025. Microsoft Office 2019 was released on September 24, 2018, and will be supported through October 14, 2025. During the supported time frame, your software licenses will include FREE updates for performance AND security.

After this time, the software will continue to function, but you won't receive any updates. Cybercriminals are aware of this, and they take advantage of the fact that many people are slow to move to the next platform. In January of 2020, Microsoft ended support for Windows 7. This led to a massive worldwide effort to get systems upgraded to Windows 10. However, a recent report on The Verge indicates up to 100 million PCs are still running Windows 7. Ouch!

When extended support ends, users are vulnerable to security risks, and will be out of compliance for all types of compliance frameworks, like HIPAA, the myriad of state data security laws, CMMC, FTC, and others. (Stay tuned for more about regulations on Day 10)

Your WIFI technology also needs to be kept up to date. If you have a very old access point using the older WEP encryption, that's a lot easier to crack (break into) than the newer technology. Hanging on to old tech is like driving an old car – you won't have the equivalent of antilock brakes, side airbags, lane departure detection, automatic braking.

Cyber Risk and Old Technology

In 2017, the WannaCry Ransomware spread around the world crippling 300,000 computers in 150 countries. Microsoft had released the patch for the vulnerability two months before the attack began. However, there were still hundreds of thousands of unpatched systems, and even millions of unsupported Windows XP systems out there. Britain's National Health System was severely impacted by WannaCry and was forced to divert patients when they couldn't provide care.

The security landscape has heated up in recent years, but none of these principles are new. The Massachusetts Data Security Law which went into effect over ten years ago states in the computer system security requirements:

> "For files containing personal information on a system that is connected to the Internet, there must be reasonably up-

to-date firewall protection and operating system security patches, reasonably designed to maintain the integrity of the personal information."

"Reasonably up-to-date versions of system security agent software which must include malware protection and reasonably up-to-date patches and virus definitions, or a version of such software that can still be supported with up-to-date patches and virus definitions and is set to receive the most current security updates on a regular basis."

This is just an example, and your state probably has its own regulations like the California Consumer Privacy Act (CCPA), New Your State Department of Financial Services Cybersecurity Regulation (NYSDFS), Colorado Data Privacy Law, the Oregon Consumer Identity Theft Protection Act, and the list goes on.

Hanging on to old technology for too long is a risk.

Saving money by hanging on to old technology and ignoring updates can ultimately result in unintended risk and expenses. Would you want to live in an old house without smoke detectors or with old faulty wiring? Take an inventory of your tech, and if it's out of date, update, or upgrade what you have. For business applications, we recommend a hardware lifecycle of no more than five years.

And remember to properly recycle old electronics – they contain dangerous chemicals that harm the environment and can't go into regular trash. (More on that later on Day 20!)

△△△

Keep your Technology up to date.

Protect Yourself On-Line – Cyber Fit Next Steps:

✓ Have you been postponing updates? Say "yes" today to your systems' security update prompts! The updates are free!

✓ Take action to replace any active hardware older than 5 years.

✓ Upgrade or dispose of any tech that is no longer supported – do not keep past end-of-life.

✓   Protect your security and protect the environment when you dispose of old hardware. (More about the data security aspects on Day 20)

DAY #2 - STRONG PASSWORDS

"I've done my best to make your user name and password as secure as possible...but you still move your lips when you type!"

>> A **STRONG password** is a combination of random characters, numbers, and symbols that is difficult for others to guess or crack.

>> **Did you know?** The most popular passwords are "password" and "123456"

D o you use any common, easily guessable passwords like "password", "123456", "guest", "111111"? Change your password! One of the interesting by-products of a data breach is that often a "most popular password" list can be generated from the data. Most people have probably heard they need to use a strong password, but if you rely on something you can easily remember, then it's not a strong password.

There are many different reports of "most popular passwords" that all look similar. Here's a list from Nord Security, a provider of online security, reported on CNBC.

1. password
2. 123456
3. 123456789
4. guest
5. qwerty
6. 12345678
7. 111111
8. 12345
9. col123456
10. 123123
11. 1234567
12. 1234
13. 1234567890
14. 000000
15. 555555
16. 666666
17. 123321
18. 654321
19. 7777777
20. 123

10% of all passwords are either "password" or "123456". No wonder our data isn't safe! Using "Month-Year" as your password? Change it!

Recently the Department of the Interior "hacked" itself to show how easy it would be to crack employee passwords. According to the report by the Office of the Inspector General, in 90 minutes and with less than $150,000, the test obtained clear-text passwords for 16% of user accounts! In that report, the most used password was "Password-1234". This is better than past tests, where 20-40% of passwords were cracked, but still a serious risk. With vast resources, even the government isn't keeping data safe.

How long does it take to guess a password?

In a recent report from the World Economic Forum entitled "This chart shows how long it would take a computer to hack your exact password" – we can see how easy it is to crack a "weak" password.

The chart below from the report shows how much time it would take for a computer to crack your password given a combination of characters and symbols and length. Adding just one uppercase letter to a password extends the cracking time by 22 minutes. This is because when more types of characters, symbols and numbers are used, the combinations of potential passwords increase exponentially. Keep in mind that computers keep getting faster so these times will get faster, and when Quantum Computing becomes main stream it's a whole new game!

How Safe Is Your Password?

Time it would take a computer to crack a password with the following parameters

Number of characters	Lowercase letters only	At least one uppercase letter	At least one uppercase letter +number	At least one uppercase letter +number+symbol
1	Instantly	Instantly	-	-
2	Instantly	Instantly	Instantly	-
3	Instantly	Instantly	Instantly	Instantly
4	Instantly	Instantly	Instantly	Instantly
5	Instantly	Instantly	Instantly	Instantly
6	Instantly	Instantly	Instantly	Instantly
7	Instantly	Instantly	1 min	6 min
8	Instantly	22 min	1 hrs	8 hrs
9	2 min	19 hrs	3 days	3 wks
10	1 hrs	1 mths	7 mths	5 yrs
11	1 day	5 yrs	41 yrs	400 yrs
12	3 wks	300 yrs	2,000 yrs	34,000 yrs

Source: Security.org

statista

If you've ever been locked out of an account, and it wasn't you trying to get in, that could be a sign there's an attempt on your account. Password lockouts (three strikes and you're out) help protect your security by stopping brute-force break ins. Lockouts are *not* a random punishment from the IT department!

How can you make your password STRONG?

- Use *at least* 12 characters.
- Use a mix of uppercase and lower-case letters - symbols and numbers should be included
- A 12-character password with these characteristics would take a computer 34,000 years to crack (but keep in mind computers keep getting faster!)

Passphrase

One strategy to create a strong password is to use a "passphrase" which is a sentence like sting of of words that is a lot longer than a traditional password, but easier to remember. Keep in mind though that they still need to contain uppercase, lower case, numbers and symbols. You can start with a simple sentence like "Winters in Massachusetts are cold" and work from there by substituting some characters for letters.

What we KNOW and what we DO

Strong passwords are something you've probably heard about before and maybe you're clear on what you "should" do about passwords, but reality is quite a bit different as a recent report by LogMeIn shows (in collaboration with the National Cybersecurity Alliance). Most people believe they are knowledgeable about the risks of poor password security; however, they're not *using* that knowledge to protect themselves from cyber threats. Good password hygiene is one of the most important steps you can take to secure your data.

It's kind of like flossing your teeth - you know you should do it, but if you don't, you put your dental health at risk. You'll start seeing a theme here … security requires your *participation*!

LastPass, a provider of password protection security software, put together a report on the **Psychology of Passwords**. Here are some of the key take away's:

- 91% of computer users know that using the same or variation of a password is a risk, but 66% do it anyway.
- 54% of computer users try to keep track of passwords by memorizing them and it's not working. 24% of them need to reset passwords monthly after forgetting.
- The old advice of 8 characters for a strong password is out of date - the longer the better and in this case, eight is not enough.
- 52% of computer users haven't changed their password in a year even after learning of a breach!
- Don't re-use passwords. Keep in mind that hackers can use "credential stuffing" to try to use your password at all the other sites where you may use it. If your Facebook password is compromised, and you use the

same password at your bank, you've just put your bank account at risk too! With automated tools, credential stuffing is a quick task! And now, these automated tools are becoming even smarter with the integration of AI.

The typical 90-day forced password reset policy can make passwords less secure. Why? Users will fear forgetting their password and will quickly take on some other bad habits like writing them down, re-using passwords, or creating passwords that are too simple. One philosophy on passwords is to keep a password that's strong until you have reason to change it (like a publicized breach).

DON'T OVERSHARE on social media.

Social media is great for a lot of things: Sharing photos, connecting with old friends, and finding like-minded people and groups to share ideas and hobbies. Social media is also widely used by businesses to market products and events, keep on top of industry trends, and prospect for new customers. But when does sharing become over-sharing and when does social media pose a risk?

Hackers can gain access to your personal data via your profile and the information you share there. Your mother's maiden name, the high school you graduated from, your nickname, college mascot, your first pet?... These are common password challenge questions ("secret questions"). Don't make it easy for your accounts to get compromised!

Watch out also for those fun quizzes online. Many are just avenues to harvest your personal information. The seemingly amusing quiz that reveals your information or tests how well you know a friend might not be so innocent. First job? Favorite TV Character? Favorite Band? Think twice before participating.

Get to know the privacy settings on your account, and keep in mind that these often change with no warning with various updates. If you're headed away for vacation, consider waiting for your return before posting so you don't tip off criminals that your home is vacant.Speaking of travelling, don't share a photo of your boarding pass. The barcode on the boarding pass contains your full name, flight information, and airline account number. Small pieces of information that may not seem important on their own can be pieced together to guess your login information, or even create a fake account in your name.

Is social media a data breach risk? It can be. Here's a few things you can do to fight back:

- Enjoy social media but remember to think before you post! This is probably the single most important factor.
- Be aware of impersonated profiles. Is the person you're connecting with really who they say they are?
- Always use STRONG passwords and consider Dark Web monitoring (more on "Dark Web" in Day 3) to help ensure your credentials haven't been leaked.
- Monitor your accounts for any suspicious activity, in particular fake posts in your name.
- Watch for spear-phishing emails (more on this in Day 6) or messages asking for credentials or other information - think before you click!

The more you know about the different types of risks, the safer you'll be online. As social media continues to gain popularity for both personal and business applications, it will become increasing popular for cybercriminals to use social media in their attacks. Acting now to become more cyber-aware, and safeguarding your information will help prevent social media from becoming a source of trouble for you.

$$\triangle\triangle\triangle$$

Strong Passwords

Protect Yourself On-Line – Cyber Fit Next Steps:

- ✓ Did you recognize any of your passwords on the most popular passwords list? Put the book down and change any of those passwords RIGHT NOW!

✓   Use STRONG passwords: A combination of uppercase and lowercase letters, numbers, and symbols at least 12 characters long.

✓ Don't re-use passwords across different sites or recycled for the same site.

✓   Change password when a breach occurs – (and this is why you don't use a PW across multiple sites). If one of companies you do business with like Target, or Chase Bank gets breached, change your password. Keep up with the news headlines.

✓   Don't overshare on social media – criminals can use this information to potentially access our accounts.

DAY #3 - PASSWORD MANAGER

"Sorry about the odor. I have all my passwords tattooed between my toes."

>> A **password manager** is a software application designed to store and manage online credentials (usernames and passwords)

>> **Did you know?** The average person needs 50-100 passwords.

We've established the need for STRONG and UNIQUE passwords, and can you spot the problem? How can anyone remember all these passwords, and change them frequently enough?

The average person uses 50-100 different accounts online. How can anybody memorize all those strong and unique passwords? Think of all the places you login: your bank, Netflix, Facebook, Verizon, your school, your utilities, and the list goes on... Unless you're a Guinness Book of World Records memory expert, you'll wind up with some bad password habits – reusing passwords, short passwords, passwords written on post-its, or the little notebooks you can find in some gift shops, etc.

Psychology of Passwords:

We tend to think that re-using passwords gives us control because we can remember them, but it puts us at risk. As more and more people work and socialize online, hackers are looking for opportunities to take advantage and steal personal information. Unless you're a superhero, there's just no way to memorize strong and unique passwords for all the sites we work with. A recent survey from LastPass by LogMeIn of over 3,000 people revealed some very important trends about passwords:

- 60% of people surveyed reported they are afraid of forgetting passwords.
- Memorizing passwords doesn't work - it's just not possible to keep track if you are using strong, unique passwords on all of your accounts. 25% of people reset passwords at least once a month because they forgot them.
- We use the same password over and over - if a hacker gets access to ONE password, they have access to MANY accounts. 91% of people know that re-using passwords is a mistake, but 66% do it anyway.
- We ignore breaches - 52% of people reported not changing a password in over 12 months AFTER knowing about a breach.
- We're predictable - 22% could guess the password of their significant other.

Password managers are software tools that address the balance between the need for strong passwords and the convenience of having them available when you need them (and not locked up in a Bank Safe Deposit Box). Password managers also include password generators to create strong passwords of a desired length and complexity. Some of the popular password managers on the market include – LastPass®, NordPass®, Dashlane®, and Keeper®. A lot of people store passwords in their browser, like Chrome®, because it's convenient, but this is NOT secure. Use an actual business-class password manager.

The biggest concern we hear is about putting "all eggs in one basket". Password managers are designed with this risk in mind. Passwords are encrypted and stored in a software vault, so if someone got access to the vault data, they could not actually see your password without the decryption key. If you use a password manager, it is *critical* that you have a very strong password for the vault (and multifactor authentication, which we'll cover in the next session). There's no such thing as zero risk, but the risk of weak and re-used passwords is far greater than the risks inherent in password managers.

Weak passwords account for the majority of data breaches. 60% of small and medium businesses (SMBs) have no visibility into employee password habits and have no password policies. Almost two thirds of employees in SMBs use the exact same password for everything. If you own a business, do you know how well your employees are doing with password hygiene?

Passwords wind up on the Dark Web.

Even with STRONG passwords facilitated by a business-class password manager, through no fault of your own, your passwords could still wind up exposed on the Dark Web. If a company you work with has a breach, your password may be exposed and sold by credential brokers. Third-party application breaches can result in password exposure while additional cyberthreats, such as keystroke logging or brute force attacks, can be used to systematically identify or capture even the most complex passwords.

What is the Dark Web? The Dark Web is a term used to describe a collection of websites that exist on an encrypted network and can only be accessed using specialized software, such as the Tor®

browser. These websites are not indexed by search engines and are typically used for illegal activities such as the sale of drugs, weapons, and stolen data, as well as for enabling anonymous communication and the sharing of sensitive information. It is important to note that while some of the content on the Dark Web is illegal, there is also a lot of legitimate activity that takes place on these networks, such as whistle-blowing and political activism.

In the iceberg analogy of the Dark Web, we see that about 4% of all Internet traffic involves the public websites we use every day like google.com, cnn.com, yahoo.com, weather.com, etc. The *Deep* Web is defined as everything on the web that's protected with passwords – you can't get to the contents without appropriate credentials, including things like medical records, financial records, legal records, government reports, subscription services, etc. The *Dark* Web is deeper than the deep web, and requires special technology to access. It's also where the criminals operate.

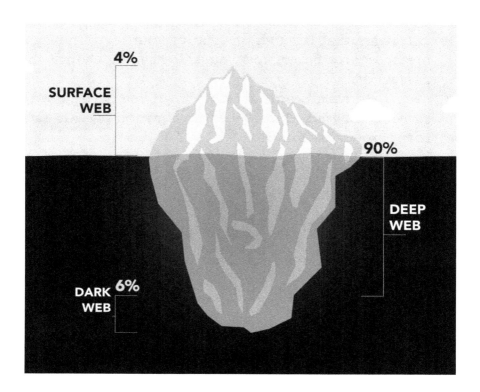

Dark Web Research:

Knowing in real-time what passwords and accounts have been compromised and posted on the Dark Web will allow you to be proactive in preventing a data breach. Its creepy to think about, but your stolen credentials may have been posted for sale. Your password manager will alert you to that.

$$\triangle\triangle\triangle$$

Password Manager:

Protect Yourself On-Line – Cyber Fit Next Steps:

- ✓ Use a password manager to facilitate good password hygiene (strong, unique passwords).
- ✓ Be aware of the limitations of a password manager – there is a risk, but the risk of weak passwords is greater. Use a VERY STRONG vault password (with Multi Factor Authentication which we'll review in the next chapter).
- ✓ Be aware that through no fault of your own, third-party breaches may occur, and you will need to change those passwords.
- ✓ Don't store passwords in browsers. If you have passwords saved in browsers, change the password and DO NOT save it to the browser again.

DAY #4 MULTI FACTOR AUTHENTICATION

© Glasbergen/ glasbergen.com

"If you were concerned about identity theft, you shouldn't have left your private information lying around where I could find it!"

>>**Multifactor Authentication (MFA)** is an authentication technique that requires users to have two or more verification methods to get access to an account.

>>**Did you know?** If you get a request to "approve" a multifactor authentication request that you didn't initiate, someone passed the first challenge and knows your password.

Multifactor authentication (MFA) is an important security solution, part of a layered security plan where the system requires the user to present more than one set of credentials to be verified. MFA increases security because if a password is compromised, unauthorized users will be unable to meet the second authentication. Remember the TV show Get Smart and all those doors at the beginning of the show? If an intruder gets through one door (a password), they would still be locked out without having the second method of authentication. You've also probably also heard the term Two Factor Authentication(2FA) which is a type of MFA in which two layers of security are used (two unique credentials required).

Multifactor Authentication methods are based on three types of information:

1. Things you **know**: Password, PIN, answers to security challenge questions.
2. Things you **have**: cell phone (receive a text message), one time passcodes, badge or key
3. Things you **are**: biometrics – fingerprint, iris scanning, face recognition

Here's how it works. When you log into a website, you'll be prompted for your username and password. If these are correct, then you'll be asked for additional information. You may have seen a message "we don't recognize this computer" when you log into your bank. That's because it's checking your IP address, or settings on your system as a passive type of two factor authentication based on location and settings. Alternatively, you may be emailed or texted (typically) a six-digit code, or you may have what's known as an authentication app (Duo®, Google Authenticator®) that generates a code for you, or presents a pop up on your phone to "approve" the login.

Even with a STRONG and unique password, it's possible that your password could be compromised through no fault of your own if there's a breach somewhere. For example, Capital One® had a breach in 2019, and as a result, millions of their customers' passwords were leaked. LinkedIn® and Yahoo® have had breaches as well, and the list goes on. Best practice is to change your password when you hear of a breach like this, but you may not have heard the news, or like many people, just didn't bother changing the password. In this case, without two factor authentication, a hacker could get right into your account.

With the extra protection of two factor authentication, it is extremely unlikely that someone could get in. While there are sophisticated ways that some multifactor authentication methods can be broken, this is a high hurdle and there is plenty of lower hanging fruit for the criminals to pursue.

By the way, have you ever received a multifactor authentication message and you weren't trying to log in? It could mean a few things. First, it's possible that someone actually got into your account past the username and password, and then got blocked when the two-factor challenge came up (YOU got the code, not them). Also watch out that it could be a phishing attempt. A FAKE message designed to alarm you that someone is trying to get into your account, and trick you into logging in.

There's even a phenomenon called "MFA Fatigue" – people get so many messages from their many login activities and just hit "accept" to clear one more message among many, when in fact they may have inadvertently replied to a spoof from a bad actor. The social engineering cyber-attack strategy is also known as MFA Bombing, or MFA Spamming.

Yes, MFA is inconvenient, but do it anyway.

It can seem inconvenient, but it is EXTREMELY IMPORTANT that you enable multifactor authentication everywhere you can. Yes, it will slow you down a bit, but it makes it almost impossible for someone else to get into your account. Most places REQUIRE MFA now, but if you're given a choice, INCREASE your security by turning it on.

Microsoft published an interesting piece in the Tech Community "Your Pa$$word doesn't matter". We just covered the need for having a STRONG password, and what's this? It doesn't matter? Well, it does matter, BUT without Multifactor authentication, there are a lot of easy ways to get into accounts:

- **Credential Stuffing** - This is very common. When a major breach occurs that you read about in the news, for example with your credit card company, those passwords are all exposed and criminals use these to test for matches at other sites. This is why you need to use DIFFERENT passwords for each site, but in practice, most people don't. In this case, it doesn't matter how STRONG your password is, the attacker has it.
- **Phishing** - An email is received with an entertaining lure, or a threatening item like a fake big invoice. The curious user may click on the link and turn over credentials when they log in to the fake site. Doesn't matter how STRONG your password is, you just gave it to the attacker.
- **Keystroke Logging** – Certain types of malware (malicious software) can basically log and transmit everything you type, including usernames and passwords. Doesn't matter how strong your password is, the attacker can just record it.
- **Local Discovery** – This could be dumpster diving (yes – literally pawing through trash in a dumpster or trash can... people have even found Bank ATM hard drives with account number and pins), physical reconnaissance (which is rare), or network scanning (which is more common). Doesn't matter how STRONG the password is, it was found by the attacker.
- **Extortion** – A threatening phishing email will either trick you into providing credentials through logging into a fake account with your real credentials, or in some cases request payment.
- **Password Spray** – Attackers can easily get a list of passwords from exposed breaches and just try all those passwords. This is done through automation.
- **Brute Force** – Cyber criminals just try thousands of password permutations using automation. The stronger your password, the safer you'll be, but in reality, most

people don't have passwords this strong.

Password Challenge Question: Some sites use this security feature to verify a user's identity by asking them to answer a question or provide information that only they should know. Examples include "What was you first pet's name?" and "What city were you born in?". Keep in mind that these are vulnerable to social engineering attacks if the information is too publicly available. We talked previously in the Strong Passwords chapter about the risk of oversharing on social media to enable guessing passwords, and these challenge questions are also not secure enough for these reasons and not considered a substitute for MFA.

△△△

Multi-Factor Authentication (MFA):

Protect Yourself On-Line – Cyber Fit Next Steps:
- ✓ Have you skipped any requests to set up MFA? Set it up now on all your accounts!
- ✓ When possible, create an alternate verification process (e.g. an email address or voice call) in case you lose your mobile phone.
- ✓ Yes, MFA is inconvenient – do it anyway!

DAY #5 – INVENTORY AND ASSET MANAGEMENT

"How do I download something from the cloud on a clear, sunny day?"

>> Why is **Inventory and Asset Management** so important for cybersecurity? You can't protect what you don't know about.

>> **Did you know?** 32% of employees are using communication or collaboration tools at work that aren't approved by IT (*2022*

Workplace trends & insights report, Beezy)

S ounds very simple, but the starting block for the National institute of Standards and Technology (NIST) and all the security frameworks built upon those standards starts with IDENTIFY. What data do you have that you want to protect, and where is it?

The NIST Cybersecurity Framework covers five key areas: IDENTIFY – Protect – Detect – Respond- Recover. You can't know what to protect if you don't know what it is! IDENTIFY includes devices, applications, networks, data and users!

When you are securing your home, it's important to know what you have that you're protecting --the physical safety of your family members, your electronics, jewelry, family photos, etc. The same is true of your technology. What do you have and where is it located?

Digital Sprawl

With respect to your digital assets, what are you protecting and where is it? Are you storing any protected information like financial information or social security numbers? There are regulations that govern this. Is the data on multiple computers, a single computer? Have any employees made copies of the data?

Shadow IT:

Shadow IT is the use of information technology systems, devices, software, applications, and services without explicit IT department approval, like automatically forwarding emails to a personal account, storing work files on an unsecured personal laptop, or using unauthorized applications like TikTok, which the US Government has now ordered people to remove from all government issued devices. Shadow IT can be a major security risk for organizations as these systems and devices may not be properly secured or managed, and they may also be used to access or store sensitive data without the knowledge or oversight of the IT department. Additionally, the use of shadow IT can make it difficult for the organization to maintain compliance with regulations and industry standards.

Need to work late one night and plan on bringing files home or sharing them to your personal Drop Box account to access later? You may be a great employee, and going the extra mile to get work done, but you're putting your company at risk (and you may be putting your job at risk).

Often people wind up using "shadow IT" because they're frustrated with the technology available to them at work. This is a problem that needs attention, but working around the system means security oversight is lost. In a recent Forbes Insights and IBM survey, 46% of IT leaders believe the use of unsanctioned software makes it impossible to protect all their organizations, and the same survey shows that more than 1 in 5 organizations have experienced a cyber event related to Shadow IT.

You're responsible for protecting the date entrusted with you.

- **Hardware**- What is all the hardware you have – including portable hard drives and printer/scanners - that may contain data?
- **Software** – What are all the different software applications you have installed on your computer?
- **SAAS – Software as a Service** (aka online applications) What are all the online applications you use?

Data tends to move around and expand to places it doesn't need to be. All of this exposes you to increased risk.

△△△

Inventory and Asset Management:

Protect Yourself On-Line – Cyber Fit Next Steps:

✓ Take an inventory of all hardware, software, online services you use. Identify and define your assets: Determine what your critical assets are, including data, applications, systems, and endpoints. Important data may wind up where you don't expect it. Scanners, for example, can retain information on hard drives.

✓   Use software tools to search your local area network – you may find things you don't even know about.

✓   Establish protocols around shadow IT.

DAY #6 - PHISHING

© Glasbergen/ glasbergen.com

"Today at work, I received 650 E-mails from feedme@homecat.com! Was that *you?*"

>> **Phishing** is when attackers send malicious emails (or phone calls and texts) designed to trick people into falling for a scam. Analogous to the sport of fishing, phishing is a technique to "fish" for usernames, passwords, and other sensitive information from a "sea" of users. The phrase was coined over 25 years ago when hackers started stealing America Online accounts and passwords.

>> **Did you know?** 82% of breaches involved a human element (like opening an email and clicking on a bad link!) Verizon Data Breach Investigations Report.

With increasing levels of cyber protection in place, one of the best ways for cyber criminals to reach their victims is through email. As with your home security, having locks on all your doors and windows does not necessarily guarantee home security - answering the door to a stranger who might be a criminal can inadvertently compromise your safety and security. Phishing is a cybercrime in which a target or targets are contacted by email, telephone, or text message by someone posing as a legitimate institution to lure individuals into providing sensitive data such as personally identifiable information, banking and credit card details, and passwords.

Verizon reports in their 2022 Data Breach Investigations Report (DBIR) that the human element continues to drive breaches. This year 82% of breaches involved the human element. Whether it is the use of stolen credentials, phishing, misuse, or simply an error, people continue to play a very large role in incidents and breaches alike.

In Proofpoint's 2022 State of the Phish report, 83% of organizations suffered a successful email-based phishing attack in 2021, 78% of companies faced a ransomware attach that was propagated from a phishing email, while 86% experienced bulk phishing attacks and 77% sustained Business Email Compromise (BEC) attacks. Email is so central to communication, but wow, it can be dangerous!

The information obtained by phishing is then used to access important accounts and can result in identity theft and financial loss. From a cybercriminal's perspective, why go through all the effort to break in when you can just walk in the front door?

Hijacking the News

Cyber criminals have a knack for taking advantage of big holidays and major news events. During the Christmas season, there'll be a lot of scams around gift cards or holiday sales. Romance scams spike leading up to Valentine's Day. During tax season, there'll be a lot of scams around new taxes, or tax refunds. When there's a major catastrophe, criminals will post fake fundraising sites. During the early days of the Covid pandemic, phishing emails spiked when everyone was hungry for news. Remember, cybercrime is big business, so the criminals will work hard to deceive you. In 2022, Americans lost $1.3 billion to romance scams according to a Federal Trade Commission report.

Social Engineering

In the context of information security, social engineering is the use of deception to manipulate individuals into divulging confidential or personal information that may be used for fraudulent purposes, like passwords, credit card information, and more.

The many flavors of phishing emails

Spear phishing is a phishing attack targeted at a specific person or organization vs a general attack at large volumes of people. Barracuda researchers evaluated more than 360,000 spear phishing emails in a three-month period, identifying three major types of email attacks: Business Email Compromise, Blackmail, and Brand Impersonation which was the most popular with about 85% of the count. These emails are carefully designed to get through various email security technologies and effectively trick the recipient.

Business Email Compromise (BEC) - In this type of attack, the recipient will receive an email that is crafted to look like its coming from a trusted source like a supervisor, and there's typically a sense of urgency. Rarely is the actual email account taken over. It's just "spoofed" to look like it came from the boss.

From: Jane Johnson <jane.johnson@conp.com>
To: Michael Blake <michael.blake@corp.com>
Subject: Request

Hey Michael,

Are you in the office? I need to process a bank transfer for me. Give me a quick reply when you can get it done.

Regards,
Jane Johnson
CEO, Corp Corporation
Cell: 555-555-5555

The diligent employee wants to help their boss and get this done quickly, but they don't realize that they're actually sending the email to someone else when they hit "reply". This type of fraud is also called CEO Fraud, whaling, and wire transfer fraud. With so much money lost over the years, banks have started to do a great job training people to watch out for this. Watch for brevity, urgency, and pressure. Verbally confirm any instructions like this, and don't call the number in the email if one is listed.

Getting ready to buy or sell a house? Real estate transactions are usually very stressful and there's often a few last-minute glitches. This is a prime time for someone to commit fraud. Slow down and think before you click and be mindful of what you share on social media. If you post information about the property, the real estate agent who's doing such a great job, and perhaps your attorney and bank, this could be a set up for a "Business Email

Compromise" (BEC) attack. A common scam is a fake last minute wire transfer change request that looks like the real thing because the sender seems to accurately know so many details about your transaction.

The FBI reported 19,369 BEC complaints and adjusted losses of approximately $1.8 billion in 2020. Increasingly, these types of attacks are expanding from email to other messaging apps.

Brand Impersonation

In most brand-impersonation attacks, scammers use email to impersonate a trusted entity, such as a well-known company or a commonly used business application. Typically, attackers try to get recipients to give up account credentials or click on malicious links. Attackers often use domain-spoofing techniques or lookalike domains to make their impersonation attempts convincing.

Some of the most impersonated brands include:

- Microsoft®
- Apple®
- DocuSign®
- Chase®
- UPS®
- Amazon®
- LinkedIn®
- American Express®

Maybe you don't bank at Chase, for example, and that may quickly alert you that it's a fake. But you may alternatively think that someone opened an account in your name with identity theft. The bad actors can win either way. If you hover over a link (but don't click it), that may reveal the domain address of the true link. Never click on the link in the email – type your actual bank webpage into a web browser navigation bar.

Blackmail Email

Attackers frighten targets with threats containing accurate, personal information to give them credibility. They often include the victim's email address or password in the subject line. Blackmail Sextortion scams are twice as likely as Business Email Compromise attacks. Some of the subject lines may include:

- Your account has been hacked. You need to unlock.
- You are my victim.
- This is my last warning name@emailaddress.com
- Your account is being used by another person.
- Cybercriminals know your password <password> and you must change it now.

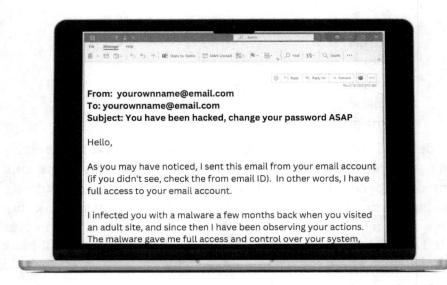

From: yourownname@email.com
To: yourownname@email.com
Subject: You have been hacked, change your password ASAP

Hello,

As you may have noticed, I sent this email from your email account (if you didn't see, check the from email ID). In other words, I have full access to your email account.

I infected you with a malware a few months back when you visited an adult site, and since then I have been observing your actions. The malware gave me full access and control over your system,

There are some technology solutions to help cut down on phishing emails (more about that later), but there's no such thing as 100% protection. However, automation tools make it easy for criminals to work with very high volumes of mail. In addition, by morphing the emails, they can bypass security filters. A combination of TECHNOLOGY solutions AND an alert user is needed.

Think before you click!

Look for the date, the from address, the to address, hyperlinks, subject attachments, content. Many email attacks include very slight misspellings. The message is often about avoiding a negative consequence or how to gain something of value. The subject may start with Re: as though the sender is replying to a message you sent, when you didn't actually send one.

Spot a Phish:

Here is an example along with some clues on how to detect that it is a phishing attack:

The subject of the email was "subscription renewal", and at the beginning of the month a lot of these may arrive in anyone's inbox. This one immediately caught my eye because the preview text showed "Hello dear". The other thing to note is that we've all been taught to not "click on the link", but this one invites us to call a number. That's a common new tactic and in the never-ending cat and mouse game as computer users become more aware of dangerous links, the cyber criminals just come up with a new twist.

Here are some more red flags about this email:

- subscription renewal - Typically the first line of an email subject would be capitalized.
- Malware Bytes - Malwarebytes is a very popular security

product, and it is ONE word, not two.

- "subscription renewal" email actually is a random gmail address. Very often these free services are abused like this. An actual renewal would be from a company domain.
- The email arrived at 4:11am. An automated batch of emails could arrive any time, but this is an unusual time especially since Monday was a holiday.
- The salutation says "Hello dear". If it were actually a renewal, they would have had a real name in the database
- "Technical Management Department" - Makes no sense.
- "You" and "Placed" are capitalized randomly.
- Product "Advance Security" - Should be "advanced"

Then they get you with the big dollar amount, and that's how they get a reaction because OF COURSE this transaction wasn't authorized. Phishing emails typically prompt some sort of urgency. Since security is such a hot topic these days, recipients may be doubly anxious to make sure all subscriptions are in order. Being savvy, they put in a phone number instead of a link so people will be tricked into thinking it's safe to call. Typically, the next step would be some attempt to get a credit card number to "refund" the charge. Don't call!

This particular email had a lot of mistakes and red flags and keep in mind that some are far better crafted and harder to spot. Also keep in mind that reviewing an email like this on your computer makes things a lot easier to see than on your tiny phone display. Sending email blasts like this doesn't cost any money, and the scam works if they get a tiny percentage of recipients to call. Everyone thinks they won't fall for a scam. But imagine seeing this on your phone on a busy day where you may have a few moments between meetings, and you just want to "take care of it".

Enter AI:

Hackers love data, and in any third-party breach, a lot of

information may be shared about you that can be used against you to make even more convincing phishing emails. They may easily be able to string together details about where you work, who your boss is, personal interests, etc. Threats can be programmatically changed to help avoid detection tools as well.

Beyond Email:

Also, it's not just emails to be aware of. Watch out for texts, phone calls, fake websites and QR codes. The FBI issued a warning last summer that cybercriminals could use altered Quick Response (QR) codes to steal personal and financial information of unsuspecting customers. QR codes are all around us these days, and they're used for everything from restaurant menus to donations. During the pandemic, many restaurants began using QR codes in place of paper menus, but keep in mind that someone could alter the code by just putting another sticker on the table.

△△△

Phishing:

Protect Yourself On-Line – Cyber Fit Next Steps:

- ✓ <u>Never</u> use the same password for multiple sites.
- ✓ Track the breaches you're involved with (for example your bank, or any online application you use) to know when your info is leaked.
- ✓ Don't assume an email containing personal information about you must be legitimate. As we've seen before, this could be from the Dark Web (previous breaches) or harvested from social media.
- ✓ Phishing emails may be very difficult to spot, so stay alert. Years ago, they would contain poor graphics and bad grammar. Not anymore.
- ✓ Don't overreact to emails with threatening information. More than likely they are just part of a bulk anonymous email

campaign.

- ✓ Watch for "seasonal" phishing campaigns such as tax refunds in the Spring, shopping around the holidays, and election info during election season.

- ✓ If an email is unexpected, pause before clicking.

- ✓ Don't follow the links or phone numbers in suspicious emails. Call the number on the back of a credit card or go directly to the web site in question for follow up.

- ✓ Use an email security filter to help reduce scam emails. However, remember that no spam filter is 100%. Cyber criminals work hard to get the threat through.

DAY #7 - DOMAIN REGISTRATION

©Glasbergen / glasbergen.com

"Sorry this is taking so long. My carrier is throttling my data plan."

>> **Domain registration** establishes who owns a domain. ("www.youridentity.com"). For example, Bank of America owns bankofamerica.com. If you own a domain, protect it. If you trust a domain, know that it can be hacked.

>> **Did you know?** Google Ads can be fake. Google is a trusted brand, but fake ads on Google are bought and used by criminals to scam consumers online. Fake Google ads are illegal and prohibited by the platform, but they are difficult to identify and stop unless reported.

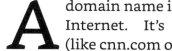 domain name is used to identify services provided on the Internet. It's an easy to read and remember address (like cnn.com or bankofamerica.com) that points a server

somewhere, that's actually identified by a bunch of numbers (an IP Address). There are two important concepts to cover here: 1) If you OWN a domain name, for example, for your local business or organization, PROTECT IT. 2) If you're a general internet user, it's important to be aware of how easy it is for criminals to trick or "spoof" people online.

A lot of people use a gmail, outlook.com, comcast.net, or verizon.net email address for their personal email, but if you run a small business or non-profit, a very important part of your branding is to establish a domain name online. The most common business domain names end in ".com" (which accounts for over 50% of all domain names) and for non-profits, ".org" (which accounts for about 5% of domain names). But did you know that there are now 300 domain suffixes? Some of the other most popular domain extensions include .net, .tv, .ai, .wtf, .lol, .fail, .eurovision, .beer, and countries: .ru (Russia), .cn (Canada), etc. Your domain name makes it easy for people to find you online, so choose something that's short, descriptive, and easy to remember.

Domain Registrar

A domain name is selected and purchased through a Domain Registrar. One of the most popular is Network Solutions, which is the one we typically recommend, but other popular registrars are GoDaddy, Google Domains, Tucows, and many more.

WHOIS

ICANN (the Internet Corporation for Assigned Names and Numbers) is a non-profit organization committed to maintaining several databases associated with domain names. ICANN is committed to maintaining the WHOIS directory, which is a public directory of contacts associated with all domain names - much like a telephone book. For the information to be useful, it must be up to date, and anyone who registers a domain name must agree to keep the information up to date. Domain name registrants, businesses, individuals, consumers, and law enforcement are all stakeholders in this directory.

As part of your contractual agreements when you registered your domain name, you agreed to keep the contact information accurate and current. If you don't want your contact information to be public, you can choose to have a private registration, but you must keep the contact information current at your registrar (behind the scenes). Note that all your renewal notices, etc, will be sent to the current contact on file, so it's also in YOUR interest to keep the information current. Even if you have a credit card on file for automatic renewal, if the card expires or gets replaced, without accurate contact information you won't get the notification and you could lose your domain name.

To look up the contact information for your domain (or any domain), go to the WHOIS database online. The registrant organization should be your *company* name. A common misstep we often see is listing an employee or a webmaster as the owner of the domain, and if you have a falling out, you may wind up losing your company's domain name. Who owns the domain? – It's very important that the information is accurate. Don't be intimidated by the jargon and let someone steal your domain. Also check that the registrant, administrative, and technical contacts are all current. If you registered your domain before you started your business, you may find that you have a very old address listed. Update it! If you're starting up a new business, WHOIS will also let you see if your preferred domain name is available.

Manage your domain.

Keep track of when your domain is up for renewal and consider having an alternate payment method online for automatic renewal. Most domain names can be registered for 1 to 10 years. Typically, there's a 30-day grace period to retain your domain if you accidently let it expire, but keep in mind that ANYONE can get it after that. Check the terms of service at your Registrar carefully.

Your Registrar is also where you can establish your Name Servers, which translate the domain name to an IP address where your website is hosted, and also direct email to the right location (DNS settings). We won't go into all the technical details, but you can see that the main thing is that if someone gets control of your domain name, possibly because you let it expire, or didn't establish proper ownership, or didn't safeguard your credentials with a strong password and MFA, they can basically take over your online identity and do whatever they want. This is important for both domain owners and consumers to know.

Laws and security make it harder for businesses to send emails.

As more and more people increase their email security, keep in mind that there are some advanced DNS settings that you will need to adjust to help ensure mail delivery. The most common are SPF records (Sender Policy Framework) that authorize your domain to send mail from Google, Microsoft, or other services like HubSpot and Constant Contact for marketing emails. We get questions about this a lot from local businesses – some of their clients receive their mail and others don't. Setting your policies properly will help deliverability. Like all things related to cybersecurity, as threats increase, protections must also increase, and there are more hurdles for legitimate Internet users.

Devious domain impersonation tricks used by criminals.

You may be wondering what you need to worry about if you're just a consumer and you don't own a domain name for a business or organization. You can see from the comments above that bad actors can potentially hijack a domain. They can take advantage of loopholes to impersonate websites and email senders, for example by creating a domain name that's very similar to a bank or other trusted service provider – known as a lookalike domain. Computers do exactly what you tell them to do – if "Bank of Ameriica" has an extra "i" in the domain, that's a different identity than the real bank.

Look alike domains are a problem for security!

Cybersquatting is the practice of registering a domain name like starbucks.org if it hasn't already been registered by the trademark owner. Watch for misspellings, typos, and look a-likes (a 1 for an "i" or an rn for an "m")

Examples: Wa1mart.com vs Walmart.com; 1kea.com vs ikea.com; bankofamerica.com vs bankofameriica.com

If you own a domain, consider purchasing a couple of other similar domain names such as common misspellings to keep someone else from getting these and potentially tricking others.

Stay alert online!

ΔΔΔ

Domain Registration:

Protect Yourself On-Line – Cyber Fit Next Steps:

- ✓   If you own a domain name, protect it by ensuring your information is kept up to date for renewals, and you protect the account with MFA.
- ✓   Watch out so you don't get tricked by similar domain names – a common technique used by criminals is to register a similar sounding domain name to one of your favorites – check the spelling carefully. Also watch for an alternative ".net" or foreign domains like .ru or .cn when you're not expecting them.

DAY #8 - EMAIL SECURITY

© Glasbergen/ glasbergen.com

GLASBERGEN

"It's the healthiest computer we sell. It works with low-sodium spam and sugar-free cookies."

>> **Email security** is important because malicious emails are a popular medium for spreading ransomware, spyware, worms, different types of malware, social engineering attacks like phishing and spear phishing emails, and other cyber threats.

>> **Did you know?** 90% of cyber threats enter organizations through email.

The typical email inbox contains a lot of clutter and even the occasional gross spam message. A cluttered mailbox is a big time-waster and makes it more difficult to make good "think before you click" decisions around. Many cyber criminals use the email inbox as the "front door" of an attack – they ring the doorbell and despite all of your locks and alarm systems, you wind up letting them in.

The first line of defense is to reduce clutter. Statistics vary, but about half of all email worldwide is spam – which means unsolicited bulk email. Unsolicited means that the recipient didn't grant permission for the email to be sent. Bulk means that the message is part of a larger collection of messages that have basically the same content. Some of this mail is just plain old gross. These days, all senders of bulk mail must follow the rules – identify themselves, allow an option to unsubscribe, and have initial permission to send mail. The CAN-SPAM rules cover "any electronic mail message the primary purpose of which is the commercial advertisement or promotion of a commercial product or service" including email that promotes content on commercial websites.

You may have wanted the sales flyers from your favorite store a few years ago when you signed up with your email. Since you signed up for it, its commercial bulk mail, not spam. Since it was at one time "solicited" – you requested it. If you can "unsubscribe", they've followed the rules.

What are the rules about sending commercial emails?

Here's the rundown of the mail requirements from the FTC website:

- Don't use false or misleading header information. Your "From," "To," "Reply-To," and routing information – including the originating domain name and email address – must be accurate and identify the person or business who initiated the message.
- Don't use deceptive subject lines. The subject line must accurately reflect the content of the message.
- Identify the message as an ad. The law gives you a lot of leeway in how to do this, but you must disclose clearly and conspicuously that your message is an advertisement.
- Tell recipients where you're located. Your message must include your valid physical postal address. This

can be your current street address, a post office box you've registered with the U.S. Postal Service, or a private mailbox you've registered with a commercial mail receiving agency established under Postal Service regulations.

- Tell recipients how to opt out of receiving future email from you. Your message must include a clear and conspicuous explanation of how the recipient can opt out of getting email from you in the future. Craft the notice in a way that's easy for an ordinary person to recognize, read, and understand. Creative use of type size, color, and location can improve clarity. Give a return email address or another easy Internet-based way to allow people to communicate their choice to you. You may create a menu to allow a recipient to opt out of certain types of messages, but you must include the option to stop all commercial messages from you. Make sure your spam filter doesn't block these opt-out requests.

- Honor opt-out requests promptly. Any opt-out mechanism you offer must be able to process opt-out requests for at least 30 days after you send your message. You must honor a recipient's opt-out request within 10 business days. You can't charge a fee, require the recipient to give you any personally identifying information beyond an email address, or make the recipient take any step other than sending a reply email or visiting a single page on an Internet website as a condition for honoring an opt-out request. Once people have told you they don't want to receive more messages from you, you can't sell or transfer their email addresses, even in the form of a mailing list. The only exception is that you may transfer the addresses to a company you've hired to help you comply with the CAN-SPAM Act.

- Monitor what others are doing on your behalf. The law makes clear that even if you hire another company to handle your email marketing, you can't contract away your legal responsibility to comply with the law. Both the company whose product is promoted in the message and the company that actually sends the message may be held legally responsible.

This is what the law states, but keep in mind that criminals don't like following the law, so there's a lot of bad stuff out there.

Filter email before it gets to your inbox.

Therefore, your mail is clean on all your devices – laptop, phone, iPad – you don't need to independently filter in each location. With email filtering, incoming email is scanned against known threats, and obvious bad email is blocked, and questionable emails are quarantined. The downside is there's an extra step involved to find the occasional missing "false positive" email stuck in your quarantine, but the extra security outweighs the inconvenience.

Some good news: Spam volume has decreased as a percentage of overall mail. When I started writing my newsletter over ten years ago, SPAM counted for about 90% of all email volume and these days it's around 50%.

The World Economic Form recently posted a few fun facts about SPAM and its 40-year history. What have we learned? Here they are…

SPAM isn't new – it's been around for over 40 years! The first SPAM message was sent in 1978 by a fellow named Gary Thuerk. He pitched a product demonstration to roughly 400 prospects via ARPANET (a forerunner to the modern internet), and reaped $13 million in sales for his company. The e-marketing ploy wasn't without controversy, however, and as Thuerk himself recalls, "complaints started coming in almost immediately". He promised to never do it again.

A few Spam facts and stats.

1. Spam costs billions each year

By 2010, an estimated 107 trillion pieces of spam email were being sent each year, costing around $130 billion per year in terms of lost productivity, energy costs and increased equipment cost.

A report by the UK government finds that in 2016, fraudulent emails cost citizens an estimated £10 billion, with almost 700,000 cases of cyber fraud recorded that year. The report says there could have been as many as 1.9 million incidents.

2. Botnets boosted spamming potential

And while Thuerk may have sent the world's first spam email, the nuisance truly exploded in 2003 with the introduction of "botnets".

Botnets - a phrase that combines the words "robot" and "network" - were designed to send millions more junk emails per day than was previously possible.

A report by Eureka magazine identified a botnet known as Rustock. It's the largest botnet on record and the report says it infected over one million computers and could send 30 billion spam emails per day. It was taken down in 2011 after around five years in operation.

3. The spam capital of the world

The US is the world leader in spam, according to data from Spamhaus. The non-profit tracks spam and other related cyber threats. As of May 4, there were more than 3,000 live spam sessions in the world churning out billions of spam messages. The U.S., China, and Russia topped the list of spam creators, while the UK, Japan and Brazil were not far behind.

4. Most spam is about healthcare

Healthcare-related junk email accounted for almost 27% of the global total in 2017, the most of any content category, Statista says. Following this, Malware equated to over a quarter of all spam sent, while dating-related spam accounted for over 21%.

5. Spam isn't effective

While trillions of spam emails are being sent every year, very few have the desired effect. Tech company Oracle/Dyn says that of 350 million spam emails sent across a 26-day period during a test, click-throughs translated to just 28 sales. That equates to a sales conversion rate of .0000083% or one-in-12 million. You'd quickly fire a sales or marketing employee with that performance!

Email marketing and automation platform GetResponse also says that just 0.02% of all spam sent globally is opened. The open rate for emails we expect and have subscribed to, for example, is considerably more than this, at almost 25%.

Security protections for your email inbox include filtering for spam, phishing attempts, and email impersonation. Technology can only go so far, and your participation is needed to think before you click!

△△△

Email Security:

Protect Yourself On-Line – Cyber Fit Next Steps:

- ✓ 90% of cyber threats enter through email – Think about that every time you open your email.
- ✓ Keep your inbox de-cluttered with an email security filter - A cluttered inbox leads to mistakes.
- ✓ SLOW DOWN. Think before you click! Criminals don't need a backdoor if they can enter through the front door – Your email inbox.

DAY # 9 - ZERO TRUST

© Glasbergen/ glasbergen.com

GLASBERGEN

"To protect our network against computer viruses,
our IT Department has issued a ban on any use of
e-mail attachments. For further details, please
refer to the attached document."

>> **Zero Trust** is a security framework requiring all users, whether in or outside the organization's network, to be authenticated, authorized, and *continuously validated* before being granted or keeping access to applications and data. You may get IN to a network but you won't be TRUSTED automatically. Never trust. Always verify.

>> **Did you know?** Traditional IT network security is built on a "castle and moat" concept or "layers of defense", where it is hard to get into a network from the outside, but everyone inside is trusted.

You may have heard of Zero Trust in relation to the Colonial Pipeline Ransomware attack. After the resulting fuel shortages and chaos, the White House issued a mandate on Zero Trust architecture, requiring all federal agencies to implement the security strategy. But what does it mean?

Zero Trust has become a bit of a buzzword, but it's basically an approach to security in which there is no inherent or implicit trust. Do you know that person who clicks on every phishing email and winds up installing malware? Zero Trust stops that. It's like having multiple security guards checking everyone's ID at multiple checkpoints before entering restricted areas and while they're there. Zero Trust is a recognition that the "castle and moat" approach to security just can't keep all intruders out of a network, and it's too risky to trust a user just because they got past all the check points. Zero Trust helps ensure that only authorized individuals can access the resources, minimizing the risk of data breaches and cyberattacks. In Zero Trust, instead of trying to keep bad traffic out of the network, simply don't allow ANYTHING on the network except what you explicitly approve. It's a strategy, not a product.

The concept of Zero Trust has been around a long time, and recently gained a lot of attention with the Presidential Executive Order "Improving the Nation's Cybersecurity". The Cybersecurity & Infrastructure Security Agency defines five pillars of Zero Trust, with traditional, advanced, and optimal maturity levels for evolution. The five pillars to focus on:

- Identity (starting points are passwords and MFA)
- Devices (starting with simple inventory)
- Network/Environment (starting with just one unsegmented network)
- Application Workload (starting with local authorization)
- Data (starting with un-inventoried, unencrypted data).

You'll recognize some of the concepts from things we have already reviewed. There's a lot of overlap with layers of defense.

Default Deny and Least Privilege

The concept of "default deny" is central to Zero Trust architecture.

Understanding the technology environment in combination with the identity of users is critical for securely granting user access to resources. By implementing strict access controls, such as least privilege, whereby a user is only granted access to information they MUST HAVE to do their job, and multi-factor authentication (MFA), "implicit trust" is removed, and security enhanced while minimizing compromise to user productivity. "Default deny" is based on the principle that all network traffic, both internal and external, is considered untrusted and must be verified before access is granted. This means that instead of granting blanket access to all users and resources, access is granted only on a case-by-case basis, based on the user's identity and the sensitivity level of the resource. This use of access controls along with constant monitoring and interpretation of network activity helps to protect against cyber threats. By assuming that all traffic is untrusted, Zero Trust architecture ensures that only authorized users and devices have access to sensitive information.

Network Segmentation

Network Segmentation is also an important security concept for Zero Trust – The Marketing Department and the HR Department, for example, should be separated – No one in marketing needs access to social security numbers. In the event of a cyber incident, the "lateral movement" can be stopped. Of course, it's inconvenient to put up a lot of barriers, but data is kept safer this way. Again, this is not your IT department just trying to annoy you.

Zero Trust Security and Layers of Defense

Watch for fads in security – sometimes what's old is new again. There is no "silver bullet" for security. Multiple approaches are explored, and the threat landscape keeps changing. Focus on the basics to help reduce risk.

△△△

Zero Trust:

Protect Yourself On-Line – Cyber Fit Next Steps and Things to Know:

- ✓ Make effective use of passwords and MFA – They always matter!
- ✓ Identify and define your assets: Determine what your critical assets are, including data, applications, systems, and endpoints.
- ✓ Segment your network: Divide your network into smaller, segmented sections to limit the impact of a potential security breach.
- ✓ Implement least privilege: Limit the access of users and devices to only the resources and systems they need to perform their job.

DAY # 10 – KNOW YOUR REGULATIONS

© Glasbergen/ glasbergen.com

GLASBERGEN

"I sent my bank details and Social Security number in an e-mail, but I put 'PRIVATE FINANCIAL INFO' in the subject line so it should be safe."

>> Data protection **regulations** help protect data against corruption, compromise, or loss.

>> **Did you know?** The Privacy Act of 1974 is a U.S. Federal law establishing controls on federal agencies' collection, maintenance, use, and dissemination of personally identifiable information. That's almost 50 years ago!

In March of 2010 (a LONG time ago!), Massachusetts put into effect a Data Protection Law with the goal of reducing identity theft and online fraud. Many other states have followed with their own regulations, and a long list of industry specific regulations exist: HIPAA (Health Insurance Portability and Accountability Act), CMMC (Cybersecurity Maturity Model Certification), PCI (Payment Card Industry), and FTC Safeguards Rule, all of which have similar requirements.

If you're a consumer working with a business, ask them how they'll protect your information. If you work in a business or a non-profit, make sure you're following best practices – protect yourself, your business, your clients, and your employees!

As an example, the technology requirements for the Massachusetts Data Security Law are listed below. What I like about this regulation is that its short and easy to read. Don't get intimidated by some of the terminology – go through line item by line item as this is a great list of practices to help anyone stay safer online. If you're a volunteer at an organization and you collect payments or any personal information, this covers you! One step at a time!

Here are the eight technology requirements included in the Massachusetts Data Security Law which went into effect March 1, 2010: **201 CMR 17.00: Standards for The Protection of Personal Information of Residents of the Commonwealth.**

The goal of the law is to help prevent identity theft and we all have a role to help.

Here are the eight technology requirements included in this law and some comments in italics:

1. Secure user authentication protocols including:

(i) control of user IDs and other identifiers;
(ii) a reasonably secure method of assigning and selecting passwords, or use of unique identifier technologies, such as biometrics or token devices;
(iii) control of data security passwords to ensure that such passwords are kept in a location and/or format that does not compromise the security of the data they protect;

(iv) restricting access to active users and active user accounts only; and

(v) blocking access to user identification after multiple unsuccessful attempts to gain access or the limitation placed on access for the particular system;

Use of STRONG passwords is required (uppercase letters, lower case letter, numbers, and symbols) and NEVER put your password on a post-it by your monitor, or under your keyboard or anywhere else that's easily accessible!

2. Secure access control measures that:

(i) restrict access to records and files containing personal information to those who need such information to perform their job duties; and

(ii) assign unique identifications plus passwords, which are not vendor supplied default passwords, to each person with computer access, that are reasonably designed to maintain the integrity of the security of the access controls;

If an employee doesn't need access to protected information to do their job, make sure they can't get to it. This is very important if multiple users share a system.

3. To the extent technically feasible, encryption of all transmitted records and files containing personal information that will travel across public networks, and encryption of all data to be transmitted over a wireless network.

Do not email personal information. There are several technologies that will enable encryption of emails, or encrypted file transfer, but never send protected information in regular email.

4. Reasonable monitoring of systems, for unauthorized use of or access to personal information;

All network and server systems and many business software applications generate activity messages stored in "log files". Are your logs routinely checked? There are several great tools to help you decipher server logs to get the information you need. How do you know if someone is on your computer or network unauthorized? If you don't look, you don't know.

5.   Encryption of all personal information stored on laptops or other <u>portable</u> devices;

Laptops MUST have encryption technology if they store any protected information. Other portable devices such as flash drives and portable hard drives must also be protected.

6.   For files containing personal information on a system that is connected to the Internet, there must be reasonably up-to-date firewall protection and operating system security patches, reasonably designed to maintain the integrity of the personal information.

Keep your tech up to date – we covered this in detail on Day 1. This is central to security.

7. Reasonably up-to-date versions of system security agent software which must include malware protection and reasonably up-to-date patches and virus definitions, or a version of such software that can still be supported with up-to-date patches and virus definitions, and is set to receive the most current security updates on a regular basis.

Do you know if your security patches (Day 1) and antivirus definitions (more on this in Day 16) are up to date?

8.   Education and training of employees on the proper use of the computer security system and the importance of personal information security.

Users often break basic rules for "convenience" so they can get their work done faster. Ongoing education is needed!

Another Cybersecurity Framework you'll hear about a lot which forms the basis for many industry specific requirements is from The National Institute of Standards and Technology at the US

Department of Commerce (NIST).   The NIST Cyber Security Framework covers five areas which are the foundations of cybersecurity, helping businesses of all sizes understand, manage, and reduce cybersecurity risk and protect their networks and data. This framework is voluntary -- it's not a regulation. But it's a great tool for understanding the foundation of what's required by various regulations.

IDENTIFY – PROTECT – DETECT – RESPOND - RECOVER

Let's start with a simple analogy of home security: Think about how you secure your own home from outside threats. Everyone has doors and windows, to keep people out. People may have dead-bolt locks, security systems, motion sensors, video cameras, a fence, a big dog, etc. You get the picture. It's not just ONE thing that you do for security, it's the combination of many things put together that help keep you secure. Also, different people employ different levels of protection in order to feel safe - everyone has a different level of risk tolerance.

Think about the analogy for protecting your home – you'll note that it's not just one "thing" for each category. This is the same as "layers" of security.

Protect:
- Doors/Windows
- Locks
- Fence
- Yard Signs

Detect:
- Alarm
- Motion Sensor
- Doorbell Camera
- Neighborhood Watch

Respond:
- Dog

- Security Service
- Police

Now imagine a major crime wave hits your town and your neighborhood. Imagine that several of your neighbors have had home break-ins. At this point, most people would wisely reconsider ALL of their security options, strengthen each of their layers of protection and adding a few more. Are ALL your windows locked? Does your family know what to do when an intruder rings the doorbell? Do you have motion sensors? Is your alarm system up to date and connected to the police department? Basically, to retain your level of safety, you must respond with more security protection to address the increased threat.

Moving on to cybersecurity, we'll take the same approach of Protect, Detect, Respond, and add Identify and Recover to complete it.

IDENTIFY – PROTECT – DETECT – RESPOND - RECOVER

Identify – Remember if you don't know about it, you can't protect it! We previously introduced this, and here you see how it fits into a fancy "framework" of security.

- Make a list of all equipment, software, and data you use, including laptops, smartphones, tablets, and point-of-sale devices.
- What data are you trying to project – data owner, power users, accounting, and HR business applications
- What are the threats that could impact that data – Cyber Attack, accidental deletion intentional insider, spear phishing.
- What is your current ability to detect and respond to those threats – How much downtime can you tolerate? Lost revenue, missed opportunities, etc.
- Create and share a company cybersecurity policy that covers:
  - Roles and responsibilities for employees, vendors, and anyone else with access to

sensitive data.
- ◦ Steps to take to protect against an attack and limit the damage if one occurs.

Protect

- Control who logs on to your network and uses your computers and other devices.
- Use security software to protect data.
- Encrypt sensitive data, at rest and in transit.
- Conduct regular backups of data.
- Update security software regularly, automating those updates if possible.
- Have formal policies for safely disposing of electronic files and old devices.
- Train everyone who uses your computers, devices, and network about cybersecurity. You can help employees understand their personal risk in addition to their crucial role in the workplace.

Detect

- Monitor your computers, devices (like USB drives), and software for unauthorized personnel access.
- Investigate any unusual activities on your network or by your staff.
- Check your network for unauthorized users or connections.

Respond

- Have a plan for:
  - ▪ Notifying customers, employees, and others whose data may be at risk.
  - ▪ Keeping business operations up and running.
  - ▪ Reporting attacks to law enforcement and other authorities.
  - ▪ Investigating and containing attacks.
  - ▪ Updating your cybersecurity policy and plan with lessons learned.

- ■ Preparing for inadvertent events (like weather emergencies) that may put data at risk.
  - Test your plan regularly.

Recover

After an attack:

- Repair and restore the equipment and parts of your network that were affected.
- Keep employees and customers informed of your response and recovery activities.

We're advising all SMBs in our community to be very clear about what protection you have and what protection you don't have, so you can make informed decisions about your security gaps and risk tolerance.

Every industry may have specific standards that address their unique demands. For instance, in healthcare you need to be in compliance with The Health Insurance Portability and Accountability Act of 1996 (HIPAA). This is a federal law that provides national standards to protect sensitive patient health information from being disclosed without the patient's consent or knowledge. and we'll go into some depth here as an example. Non-compliance can result in fines enforced by the Department of Health and Human Services. HIPAA-covered entities must safeguard the Protected Health Information (PHI) of patients, strictly control when PHI can be divulged, and to whom.

Since the Enforcement Final Rule of 2006, the Office for Civil Rights (OCR) has had the power to issue financial penalties (and/ or corrective action plans) to HIPAA-covered entities that fail to comply with HIPAA Rules.

Financial penalties for HIPAA violations were updated by the HIPAA Omnibus Rule, which introduced charges in line with the Health Information Technology for Economic and Clinical Health Act (HITECH). The Omnibus Rule took effect on March 26, 2013.

The four categories used for the penalty structure are as follows:

Tier 1: A violation that the covered entity was unaware of and could not have realistically avoided, had a reasonable amount of care had been taken to abide by HIPAA Rules

Tier 2: A violation that the covered entity should have been aware of but could not have avoided even with a reasonable amount of care. (but falling short of willful neglect of HIPAA Rules)

Tier 3: A violation suffered as a direct result of "willful neglect" of HIPAA Rules, in cases where an attempt has been made to correct the violation.

Tier 4: A violation of HIPAA Rules constituting willful neglect, where no attempt has been made to correct the violation within 30 days.

In the case of unknown violations, where the covered entity could not have been expected to avoid a data breach, it may seem unreasonable for a covered entity to be issued with a fine. OCR appreciates this and has the discretion to waive a financial penalty. The penalty cannot be waived if the violation involved willful neglect of the Privacy, Security, and Breach Notification Rules.

HIPAA Violation Penalty Structure

Each category of violation carries a separate HIPAA penalty. It is up to OCR to determine a financial penalty within the appropriate range. OCR considers a number of factors when determining penalties, such as the length of time a violation was allowed to persist, the number of people affected, and the nature of the data exposed. An organization's willingness to assist with an OCR investigation is also taken into account. The general factors that can affect the amount of the financial penalty also include prior history, the organization's financial condition, and the level of harm caused by the violation.

Tier 1: Minimum fine of $100 per violation up to $50,000

Tier 2: Minimum fine of $1,000 per violation up to $50,000

Tier 3: Minimum fine of $10,000 per violation up to $50,000

Tier 4: Minimum fine of $50,000 per violation

The above fines for HIPAA violations are those stipulated by the HITECH Act. It should be noted that these are adjusted annually to take inflation into account.

Versions of the above rules and regulations exist for other specific industries and should be sourced, referenced, and followed if they apply to your business. For example, any small business that operates within the Defense supply chain will need to adhere to CMMC requirements which are just ast stringent as HIPAA. Over time, we'll see more regulations, and more fines for the failure to protect data.

△△△

Know your Regulations:

Protect Yourself On-Line – Cyber Fit Next Steps and Things to Know:

- ✓ Get acquainted with the relevant regulations that apply to both you and your business.
- ✓ Learn from these requirements – they're designed to help you stay more secure. They exist for a reason: to help improve security.
- ✓ Tackle one regulation at a time – don't get overwhelmed.

DAY #11 - CYBER INSURANCE

© Glasbergen/ glasbergen.com

GLASBERGEN

"But do you have any experience in *Internet* security?"

>> **Cyber insurance** is a type of insurance that helps businesses and individuals mitigate financial losses resulting from cyberattacks, data breaches, and other cyber incidents.

>> **Did you know?** A 2020 survey by the Insurance Information Institute found that only 47% of small businesses in the United States had cyber insurance.

If all else fails, cyber insurance will help protect your income and business with financial help in the event of a cyber incident. With cyber risk, you can avoid risk, mitigate risk, accept risk, and with insurance transfer (some of) the risk.

A small business is well-advised to get cyber insurance for protection against financial losses resulting from cyberattacks, data breaches, and other cyber incidents. Cyber insurance can cover expenses such as forensic investigations, notification costs, credit monitoring, and legal fees. It can also provide liability coverage in case a customer or third party sues the business for damages resulting from a cyber incident. With the increasing frequency and sophistication of cyberattacks, cyber insurance can provide small businesses with some peace of mind and financial protection.

A few years ago, when this was a new category of insurance it was pretty easy and inexpensive to get. With the explosion of cyber events in the past few years, the insurance has become a lot harder to get, more expensive, and more restrictive. Be prepared to fill out a long list of questions about your cyber readiness. Your insurance company will want to know if you use multifactor authentication, if you have phishing controls in place, and if you're using advanced endpoint protection. They'll also ask if you've had a cyber incident event in the past. Even if you learned your lesson the hard way and put every cyber control in place that you possibly could after your previous event, to many insurance carriers, you'll still be viewed as a risk, and may not be able to get insurance.

Note that while insurance will help you financially, and help you navigate the experience with a breach coach and forensics resources, it can't prevent cyber events and the resulting downtime and reputation loss. In January of 2023, Iowa's largest school district cancelled classes for two days after a cyberattack. The superintendent of schools said, "This is one of the reasons why we have cyber insurance. We allow the experts to guide us on the right path." Yes, cyber insurance is a big help, but that didn't change that 5,000 employees and 31,000 students in over 60 schools were out of school for two days.

Check your policy and understand the benefits. As your business grows, your coverage needs may evolve as well, so keep current. Your regular business insurance doesn't cover cyber incidents, and keep in mind that some incidents are considered "foreign acts of war" and may not be covered. It's extremely important to answer the insurance questionnaires truthfully and provide detail. There are more and more reports of claims being denied if a company didn't have the right protections in place thereby enabling a breach. Also, watch out for sub-limits. You may have a $1M policy, but only have a fraction of that coverage for Business Email Compromise, for example. Get insurance but recognize that it doesn't solve all problems.

Here's a question from a cybersecurity policy application that a client asked us to help review – you can see that insurers really want to dig in these days to understand your risk:

(1)   Do you use an endpoint detection and response (EDR) tool that includes centralized monitoring and logging of all endpoint activity across your enterprise? If "yes", complete the following:
    a. Select your EDR provider from the list, and if "other" name the supplier.
    b. Do you enforce application whitelisting /blocklist?
    c. Is EDR deployed on 100% of endpoints?
    d. Can users access the network with their own device ("Bring Your Own Device")? If yes, is EDR required to be installed on these devices?

As you can see, insurance companies are looking for a lot of detail in your responses for cyber preparedness.

Your insurance company will advise you after a cyber event to take immediate steps to contain the damage and prevent further attacks. This may involve isolating affected systems, shutting down networks, and/or restoring from backup data. It's important to document the incident thoroughly and report it to the relevant authorities, such as law enforcement and regulatory bodies, as required by law. Your insurance company may also provide you with access to cybersecurity experts and resources to assist with recovery and prevention of future incidents. It's crucial to follow their advice and guidance to ensure that you can minimize the damage and get back to business as quickly and securely as possible. Also, take care to only speak about what you *know*, not what you *think*.

I thought my IT team would take care of all this.

A lot of things that you'll need help with after a cyber event aren't something your IT team can handle. Legal advice, public relations, credit monitoring – these all require resources, and you'll need outside help. Your IT team is not tooled to do this.

Cyber Incident vs a Breach – Know the difference and use the terms carefully.

It's important also to know the difference between a cyber incident and a breach. A cyber incident refers to any cybersecurity event that *potentially* exposes a business's data or systems to damage or unauthorized access. This can include attempted or successful cyberattacks, malware infections, system failures, and other related incidents.

On the other hand, a breach refers to a specific type of cyber incident where an unauthorized person gains access to a business's sensitive or confidential information. This could include personally identifiable information (PII) of customers or employees, financial data, or intellectual property.

While all breaches are incidents, not all incidents necessarily result in a breach. For example, a cyberattack might be detected and thwarted before any data is compromised, or a system failure might cause disruption but not lead to any unauthorized access. Understanding the difference between these two terms is important for businesses to properly identify and respond to cybersecurity threats.

Budget for Left of Boom to help you Right of Boom

The terms "Left of Boom" and "Right of Boom" are used in the military to relate to activities and measures taken before or after a security incident (a "boom"). Recovering from a breach will be very expensive! After the incident, your insurance company may also drop you or raise your rates to an unattainable level. Think this through when planning your cyber defenses and be sure to put the right investment in "Right of Boom" efforts to prevent an incident. Benjamin Franklin was right: "An ounce of prevention is worth a pound of cure."

$$\triangle\triangle\triangle$$

Cyber Insurance:

Protect Yourself On-Line – Cyber Fit Next Steps and Things to Know:

✓   If you're running a local business, get cyber insurance to help protect you financially in the event of an incident. Individual insurance coverage is also becoming available.

✓ Be vigilant in managing and enhance your security practices. Insurance is NOT a replacement for good cyber controls. An insurance policy won't prevent an incident.

✓   Be prepared to handle downtime, reputation damage, and stress – these are not within the scope of cyber insurance.

✓   Review your policy to understand what's covered and what's not covered, especially sub-limits for different types of requests.

DAY # 12 – CYBER RESILIENCE

© Glasbergen/ glasbergen.com

"I'm having trouble finishing my presentation.
My computer keeps going to sleep!"

>> **Cyber resilience** refers to an organization's ability to prepare for, respond to, and recover from cyberattacks, data breaches, and other cyber incidents.

>> **Did you know?** The FBI's Internet Crime Complaint Center IC3 reported 837,376 complaints in 2021. The total losses from those complaints totaled over $6.9 billion.

Many security experts will tell you it's not a question of IF you'll experience an incident, but rather WHEN. What will you do after an event to quickly recover?

Resilience (n) The ability to recover from or adjust easily to misfortune or change (Merriam-Webster)

"Everyone has a plan until they get punched in the face." – Mike Tyson

What is an Incident Response (IR) Plan? Simply put, if there's an incident, how are you going to respond? The national cybersecurity headlines make it seem like things can't happen to "the little guy", but the reality today is that most threats are automated and non-targeted. These are just "crimes of opportunity", and everyone is at risk. While the term "Incident Response Plan" might sound intimidating, even a small number of bullets on an index card could make a big difference. The bottom line is to do SOMETHING. An overwhelmed organization will create delays and possibly more damage and lack of data availability.

Know the "Attack Vectors" for a Cyber Incident

Incidents can occur in countless ways, so it's impossible to have a detailed plan for everything. However, it's prudent to understand the most common attack vectors to begin formulating a plan.

- Email – an attack executed in an email message or attachment. Many studies estimate that around 90% of attacks occur via email.
- Web – THINK BEFORE YOU CLICK – Attacks can come from a website.
- Credentials leaked to the Dark Web.
- Brute Force – Multiple login attempts to break through
- External Media (thumb drives, etc)
- Loss or theft of equipment
- Improper usage – any incident resulting from the violation of a company's "Acceptable Use Policy" like sharing passwords or using a home computer with no security installed.

This is a pretty simple list, and a very good starting point. If you're very ambitious, MITRE ATT&CK® is a globally-accessible knowledge base of adversary tactics and techniques based on real-world observations. The ATT&CK knowledge base is used as a foundation for the development of specific threat models and methodologies in the private sector, in government, and in the cybersecurity product and service community. There are a lot of ways to attack a network, and ATT&CK is an eye chart.

How Do I Create an Incident Response (IR) Plan?

The first thing to remember about creating an Incident Response (IR) plan is that it is not a "set it and forget it" event. This is a "living" document that needs reviews and updates as changes occur in technology, your business, and your people.

The key focus on an incident response plan is to mitigate the risks of an active cyber event.

Questions and issues to consider when preparing a plan:

- Is your plan in place?
- Is your plan tested?
- Does your team know roles and responsibilities?
- Identify what is important to your company.
- Review how well your current Protect strategies are working.
- Identify gaps in your existing Protect strategies.
- Analyze Detect layer for missing items; make recommendations as needed.
- Discuss implications of current Respond capabilities and make recommendations.

A comprehensive IR plan should include:

- Identify key players within the organization, including inside and outside resources like employees, insurance agent, technical team, and legal team.
- Clearly defined roles for employees and your outside team – Use a RACI chart – Who is responsible, accountable, consulted, informed?
- Have a list of full contact information for all employees and key outside team members. This should be

accessible outside of your computer systems.
- Develop a communication plan that addresses what to say and what not to say. In a moment of crisis, scrambling only makes it worse. It is very important to know that until events are investigated and understood, speculation doesn't help.
- Where is key data stored, and how is it backed up?
- Keep an up-to-date list of your technology.
- What data and systems are most critical to the organization to keep running or recover?
- Have a communication plan to keep your team informed.
- Have a process to review "lessons learned" and use them to strengthen the plan.

Preparation is Key

Appearing unprepared to handle a crisis can cause more damage to undo, so readying the team for any call or email which lands on their desk is going to serve the entire team well in the long run.

Keep it Simple

We highly recommend a short plan that you'll be able to follow under stress, as compared to a very long and detailed plan that will just be too much to deal with in a time of crisis. "Tabletop Exercises" are simple ways to talk through what to do. Create a typical hypothetical scenario like a ransomware attack and talk through how you would respond. Basically, this is a dress rehearsal. By going through your plan on a regular basis, you'll have the opportunity to get more comfortable and prepared for the almost inevitable crisis. Start simple and take action! – again, just a handful of bullets on an index card could be a great start!

Don't Pay the Ransom - In its advisory, the Treasury's Office of Foreign Assets Control (OFAC) said "companies that facilitate ransomware payments to cyber actors on behalf of victims, including financial institutions, cyber insurance firms, and companies involved in digital forensics and incident response, not only encourage future ransomware payment demands but also may risk violating OFAC regulations."

Will you be a victim again?

ZDNET recently reported 80% of firms that choose to pay to regain access to their encrypted systems experience a subsequent ransomware attack, amongst which 46% believe it to be caused by the same attackers.

Reporting Cyber Crime:

Here are some recommendations from the National Cybersecurity Alliance. The first step to bringing cybercriminals to justice is reporting cybercrime when it happens. Cybercriminals are very hard to catch, because they can hide behind cryptocurrency, and change identities easily – closing one operation and opening another. The constant churn means law enforcement remains a step behind. Federal, State, and local authorities are raising their game to bring cybercriminals to justice.

Who to Contact – Local Law Enforcement:

Nothing can happen though if the crimes aren't reported. Even if you were the target of some sort of international sourced malware, your local law enforcement organization has an obligation to assist you by taking a formal report. They will also help make the appropriate referrals to other agencies.

The Internet Crime Complaint Center (IC3) - https://www.ic3.gov/

You can get the federal government's help with your issue by contacting IC3. IC3 is a partnership between the Federal Bureau of Investigation and the National White Collar Crime Center (funded, in part, by the Department of Justice's Bureau of Justice Assistance). IC3 will thoroughly review and evaluate your complaint and refer it to the appropriate federal, state, local or international law enforcement or regulatory agency that has jurisdiction over the matter.

Federal Trade Commission (FTC) - https://reportfraud.ftc.gov/#/

While the FTC does not resolve individual consumer complaints, it does run the Consumer Sentinel, a secure online database used by civil and criminal law enforcement authorities worldwide to detect patterns of wrong-doing. Nailing down patterns leads to investigations and prosecutions.

Keep the Evidence

That phishing email, suspicious text or ransomware isn't just bits and bytes – it's evidence. This material can help law enforcement stop and prosecute hackers.

△△△

Cyber Resilience:

Protect Yourself On-Line – Cyber Fit Next Steps and Things to Know

- ✓ Expect to have to confront a cyber incident. It's not a matter of IF, but rather WHEN it will happen.
- ✓ Have a Plan
- ✓ Revisit the Plan
- ✓ Report the Crime

DAY #13 - IOT – INTERNET OF THINGS

GLASBERGEN

"Ever since they invented cloud computing,
I keep getting data stuck between my toes!"

>> **The Internet of Things (IoT)** refers to the interconnected network of physical devices, vehicles, buildings, and other objects that are embedded with sensors, software, and connectivity to allow them to collect and exchange data.

>> **Did you know?** Many reports estimate that there will be 75 billion IoT devices by 2025.

When we think of cybersecurity, our computers and smartphones come to mind, but don't forget about all the other things connected to the Internet! Here are some of the "things" that the term "Internet of Things" refers to - There are now an estimate 17 billion IoT devices in the world packed with software that can be hacked:

- Smart thermostats, such as the Nest, that can be controlled remotely and learn your preferred temperatures.
- Garage door openers and house locks.
- Connected cars: Cars with sensors, cameras, and telematics systems to provide driver assistance, improve fuel efficiency and many other features that can connect to the internet and other devices, enabling features such as real-time traffic information, remote vehicle monitoring, and automatic emergency response. Remote theft through keyless entry systems and even remote control are new possibilities.
- Utility meters: Electric and gas meters on or in your house that enable utility companies to measure your usage remotely for billing purposes, and possibly remotely throttle usage in times of shortages.
- Wearables and fitness trackers: Devices such as smartwatches and fitness trackers that can monitor health and fitness metrics like heart rate, sleep patterns, and activity levels.
- Smart home security systems, such as the Ring and SimpliSafe, that can be controlled from a smartphone and send notifications when motion is detected.
- Smart appliances, such as refrigerators, ovens and coffee makers, that can be controlled from a smartphone and can automatically order groceries when supplies are low.
- Medical Devices – HIPAA regulations cover these devices but think of the potential impact on human life if these are hacked: blood pressure monitors, blood glucose

monitors, medication dispensers, just to name a few.
- Industrial Internet of Things (IIoT) such as predictive maintenance sensors in manufacturing and transportation equipment
- Smart irrigation systems, using weather forecast and soil moisture sensors to adjust the watering schedule.
- Smart street lighting systems with adaptive control and reporting capabilities to reduce energy consumption.
- Industrial tracking devices that can report location and temperature for high value or environmentally vulnerable product shipments.
- Personal tracking devices such as Tile, Apple Air Tag, and Samsung Galaxy SmartTag, that can be attached to people and things to track their location in real time from your Smart Phone.

If it connects to your network, it has a potential security risk. Recently, the robotic vacuum cleaner Roomba, created by iRobot, confirmed that sensitive images taken by the vacuum cleaner had been leaked online. As the robot vacuum cleaner "learns" its most efficient route, the use of cameras can potentially cause a risk. This particular incident, although involving test units rather than retail units, does highlight the potential risks that exist.

These are just a few examples of the many IoT devices that are currently available or in development. The list will continue to evolve as the technology advances and more and more devices become connected to the internet.

Some security experts see an inflexion point as attacks move from shutting down computers and stealing data to attacks that can disrupt everyday life. A recent article posted on CNBC sums it up: "The Dark Web's criminal minds see Internet of Things as the next big hacking prize". According to the Microsoft Digital Defense Report: "While the security of IT hardware and software has strengthened in recent years, the security of Internet of Things (IoT) … has not kept pace". Attacks on IoT devices can also be entry ways for attacks on critical infrastructure like electricity grids and water supplies. Large scale attacks are also a possibility, leveraging unpatched vulnerabilities in IoT devices . We're seeing products evolve and new products emerge to help protect and control devices so they can't be used for unwelcome purposes. For example, when multiple press reports highlighted incidents of stalkers hiding Apple Airtags on the clothing or vehicles of their prey, Apple enhanced their software to provide you an alert when an Airtag is tracking with your movements.

The challenges are new, and the regulations are piecemeal. Who updates their garage door opener? Addressing vulnerabilities in the field after devices are deployed is a problem and many are calling for more work to be done about security in the design phase when products are under development – make products that are securable.

△△△

Internet of Things (IoT):

Protect Yourself On-Line – Cyber Fit Next Steps and Things to Know

- ✓ Keep an inventory of EVERYTHING you own that's connected to the Internet. Take a walk around your home and office; you may be surprised how many connected devices you find.
- ✓ Change default passwords.
- ✓ Update firmware when available.
- ✓ Use a separate guest network for IoT devices.

DAY #14 – BACKUPS

© Glasbergen/ glasbergen.com

"We back up our data on sticky notes because
sticky notes never crash."

>> A **backup** is a digital copy of computer data that is taken and stored safely away from the original system for safety.

>> **Did you know?** According to the World Backup Day website (yes, it exists!) 21% of people have never backed up their data.

A data backup protects against data loss. Data loss can happen due to various reasons such as hardware failure, software corruption, accidental deletion, natural disasters, and cyberattacks. Having a backup of your data means that you have a copy of your important files, documents, and information that you can restore in case the original data is lost or destroyed. This ensures that you will not lose your important data and can continue your work, even if something happens to your computer or the original files.

When disaster strikes (large or small), two important elements contribute to your ability to recover: 1) recovery point objective (RPO), and 2) recovery time objective (RTO)

Recovery Point Objective (RPO):

This relates to the amount of data you will lose. If for example you have a computer crash on a Wednesday afternoon, and you didn't back up since the previous Friday, you'll lose five days worth of data. This is why the frequency of backups is important. Automation helps make frequent backups easier. You can only recover data included in your most recent backup.

Recovery Time Objective (RTO):

This relates to how long it will take you to restore the data. You may have an up-to-date backup in the cloud, but downloading the data may take a week, so it would take a week to recover in that case – that's your downtime.

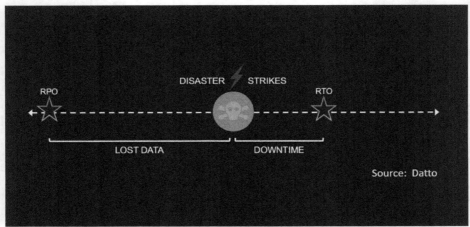

CIA – Not just a government agency!

In the context of data backup, the CIA triad refers to measures to ensure the confidentiality, integrity, and availability of data.

- **Confidentiality** refers to protecting sensitive information from unauthorized access, disclosure, or use.

- **Integrity** refers to the accuracy and reliability of information, as well as the prevention of unauthorized modification, deletion, or corruption. Backup and disaster recovery are key part of this.
- **Availability** refers to ensuring that information and computer systems are accessible and usable by authorized users when needed. Data backup, disaster recovery planning, and redundancy are a key part of this.

When evaluating different backup strategies, it's important to consider both the recovery point objective AND the recovery time objective.

Image vs "File and Folder"

An image backup creates a complete copy of an entire system, including the operating system, system settings, applications, files, and data. This means that if a system fails, an image backup can be used to restore the entire system to a previous state, including all installed applications and settings.

On the other hand, a file and folder backup only backs up specific files and directories, such as documents, photos, and other user-generated data. This means that if a system fails, a file and folder backup can be used to restore only the selected files and directories.

Image backups are typically used for disaster recovery purposes, as they provide a complete copy of the system that can be restored in the event of a catastrophic failure. File and folder backups are more commonly used for day-to-day backup and recovery needs, as they allow users to easily restore individual files and directories without the need to restore the entire system.

As with so many things in cybersecurity, there's a notion of "good", "better", "best" (and that bar keeps rising).

Good: ANY backup is better than no backup. Keep in mind that doing a very basic backup of copying files to a hard drive, runs the risk of dropping the hard drive, or just forgetting to run the backup.

Better: Automation is better than a manual backup; An image backup is better than file and folder (you may forget to cover important files with file and folder)

Best: The ability to do an instantaneous failover is the best. Typically, when we set up a backup for a local business running an important line of business application, that's what we'll recommend. It includes automated, frequent backups (so you don't lose data), and failover to redundant hardware (so you don't risk downtime). This kind of protection costs more, but it may be cheap compared to the cost of downtime and lost data.

Also, remember to **TEST your backup**. At least occasionally, test the recovery of a file.

What backup is right for you? On an index card, write down what data is most important to protect, how much data you'll tolerate losing, and how much downtime you can tolerate – these will guide you to the best backup option. Often the "3-2-1" rule for data backup is discussed – this means three copies of your data, two different media, and one off site.

Microsoft 365

One of the questions we get all the time is "do I need to backup my Microsoft 365 account? The answer is yes! Here's what Microsoft says in their service agreement under "Service Availability":

> *We strive to keep the Services up and running; however, all online services suffer occasional disruptions and outages, and Microsoft is not liable for any disruption or loss you may suffer as a result. In the event of an outage, you may not be able to retrieve Your Content or Data that you've stored. We recommend that you regularly backup Your Content and Data that you store on the Services or store using Third-Party Apps and Services.*

Cloud backups also protect against insider threats – intentional deletion of data. As if it's not enough to have to worry about cyberattacks and equipment failures, yes, insider threats are a real concern.

△△△

Data Backup:

Protect Yourself On-Line – Cyber Fit Next Steps and Things to Know

- ✓ Identify your most important data.
- ✓ Decide how much data you can tolerate losing.
- ✓ Decide how much downtime you can tolerate.
- ✓ Set up an appropriate backup that covers your needs.
- ✓ TEST your backup by trying to recover a file.

DAY # 15 – ENCRYPTION

"We've devised a new security encryption code.
Each digit is printed upside down."

>> **Encryption** is the process of converting plain text or data into a coded message that is unintelligible to unauthorized parties.

>> **Did you know?** Only 42% of companies use encryption to secure customer data – 2021 Entrust Global Encryption Trends Report.

Encryption plays an important role in cybersecurity. Encryption is a way of protecting information by converting it into a code that can only be read by someone who has the key to decrypt it – like a secret decoder ring. This makes it difficult for anyone who intercepts the information to read it, as they would not have the key to decrypt it. Encryption is commonly used to protect sensitive information, such as credit card numbers and personal information, when it is being transmitted over the internet or stored on a computer.

Encryption and Password Protection are different standards.

In both cases, a passphrase is used to unlock the data, but think of password protection as a padlock that protects your treasure chest of important information. If someone opens the padlock, all the enclosed information would be available to them. Encryption on the other hand, is like having a magic wand where the contents of the treasure chest are completely cross shredded and only the magic wand can unscramble them. If anyone could access the inside of the treasure chest, the contents would be useless.

Full Disk Encryption

All portable devices should be protected with encryption. If you were to lose your laptop, no one could access the data without the encryption key. This is also important for compliance reasons. If your laptop contains protected information, the loss doesn't have to be reported as a breach (check the specifics relating to regulations for your specific industry). Without encryption, your hard drive could just be removed from your system, and the contents easily read. There was a famous case a few years back of a Blue Cross employee who had a database of doctors on a laptop that was stolen from the back of a car -- a major security incident, that could have been prevented with simple encryption.

Encrypted Email

When you send an email, it's like mailing a postcard. It will get to the recipient, but it can easily be read along the way. NEVER email PII (Personal Identifiable Information) – financial information, account numbers, credit card numbers, passport numbers, passwords, and social security numbers. If you're using Microsoft Office 365 for email, it's easy to add a license to enable email encryption.

Encrypted Internet Connections

A secure website address (URL) should begin with "https" rather than "http." The "s" in "https" stands for secure (HyperText Transfer Protocol Secure), which indicates that the site is using a

Secure Sockets Layer (SSL) Certificate. This lets you know that all your communication and data is encrypted as it passes from your browser to the website's server. In Google Chrome, you'll see a "lock" icon for Secure, an "info" icon for Not Secure or Information missing, or a Red Exclamation mark for Not secure or dangerous.

Encrypted Doesn't Mean Safe

HTTPS – Just because you see the "lock" icon doesn't mean a website is safe!

It's important to know the "s" means the data is encrypted, but not necessarily safe! Cyber criminals abuse tools used for security and in a 2019 report by the Anti-Phishing Working Group, 58% of phishing attacks used HTTPS. Security certificates used to be expensive, but now they're low cost and sometimes even free. This makes it easier for cybercriminals to abuse HTTPS for hiding malware, ransomware, zero-day attacks, and phishing attempts. The seemingly authentic bank website could be a fake. The lock does NOT mean the site is safe, just that the traffic is encrypted – the criminals will steal your information anyway!

$$\Delta\Delta\Delta$$

Encryption:

Protect Yourself On-Line – Cyber Fit Next Steps and Things to Know

- ✓ Never email protected information – it's the equivalent of sending very private information on a postcard.
- ✓ The "S" in HTTS:// means traffic to a website is encrypted, but with low cost and free security certificates widely available, know that it doesn't mean the site is safe (criminals love this trick!).

DAY #16 – ANTIVIRUS AND ENDPOINT DETECTION AND RESPONSE (EDR)

© Glasbergen/ glasbergen.com

"We've established new security standards in the office, so don't forget to use the ecret-say ode-cay."

>> **Antivirus and endpoint detection and response** are two types of cybersecurity tools used to protect devices and networks from malware and other cyber threats.

>> **Did you know?** The first computer virus appeared over 50 years ago!

Antivirus protection is an essential tool for securing your computer and protecting your personal information. It helps to protect your computer from malicious software ("malware"), such as viruses, Trojan horses, worms, and spyware, which can harm your computer and steal your personal information.

Viruses can spread through various means such as email attachments, infected software, or even visiting a compromised website. Once a virus infects your computer, it can cause it to crash, slow down or even steal personal information. Antivirus software can detect and remove malicious software, preventing harm to your computer and personal information.

Microsoft Windows Security is built-in to Windows and includes an antivirus program called Microsoft Defender. Windows Defender is a good enough choice for basic protection against malware, but it's a good idea to get more comprehensive device protection from a solution specifically designed for security. Some examples of top antivirus solutions include Norton, Webroot, ESET, Trend Micro, and Sophos.

"I'M THE CREEPER. CATCH ME IF YOU CAN".

Computer viruses have been around for a long time. The "Creeper" program is often considered the first virus and was actually designed as a security test in 1971 by a researcher at BBN to see if a self-replicating program was possible. It had no malicious intent and only displayed a simple message "I'M THE CREEPER. CATCH ME IF YOU CAN". Originally any viruses would be limited to floppy disks and a local network, but with the widespread adoption of broadband networks during the .com age, the ILOVEYOU virus hit the world in May of 2000 and was the first widespread virus.

It became important to have antivirus software on your system, and in the early days, they worked on "definitions". As a new virus was discovered, it was added to the dictionary of viruses your software would protect you from. A "Zero Day" threat is one that hasn't been seen before, and therefore wouldn't have protection. As is always the case in cybersecurity, this became a bit of a cat and mouse game, and the bad actors would introduce polymorphic viruses – ones that change so they never look alike and you can't really protect against them with a "definition". Then "behavior" became more important.

Early viruses were designed for vandalism or reputation damage (sending an I LOVE YOU email to everyone in your contact list) – some people think that's fun. But with the introduction of crypto currency, it became easy for criminals to monetize malware through anonymous financial transactions, and that's when cybercrime really exploded.

Beyond the antivirus solutions mentioned earlier, even better security can be achieved with Endpoint Detection and Response (EDR) system. And EDR system automatically detects threats in real time that have bypassed other security tools (remember no single layer is 100% defective) by looking at behavior, like an unexpected registry change (that's a change deep in your computer's code).

While Antivirus works like a bouncer to keep people out of an establishment, EDR is more like a security system to see what they're doing if they get in, like unlocking a back door to break in later. Like all things cybersecurity, as the threat level increases, the level of protection to stay safe also increases. Proactively hunting for threats, real-time visibility, and accelerated response to incidents are all reasons to implement an EDR solution.

Some of the popular EDR solutions include: Sentinel One, CrowdStrike.

There's a lot of chatter these days about the power of AI tools like ChatGPT to develop new malware or new phishing campaigns. Hackers can create AI-powered, situationally aware and highly evasive malware and ransomware that can analyze the target system's defense mechanisms, and quickly learn and mimic normal system communications to evade detection.

Protection may range from good, better, best... and best is a changing bar. But remember, good is a great place to start!

$$\triangle\triangle\triangle$$

Anti-Virus and Endpoint Protection:

Protect Yourself On-Line – Cyber Fit Next Steps and Things to Know

- ✓   Confirm you are running antivirus software. Microsoft Windows Defender is a good basic antivirus tool.
- ✓   Confirm your antivirus software is active and up-to-date. Commercial antivirus products run on a subscription model and need to be renewed.
- ✓ Consider Endpoint Detection and Response (EDR) software if you deem your environment requires more advanced and better protection.

DAY #17 - FIREWALL

© Glasbergen/ glasbergen.com

"I'm sure there are better ways to disguise sensitive information, but we don't have a big budget."

>> A computer **firewall** is a security tool that helps protect a computer or network by monitoring and controlling incoming and outgoing network traffic.

>> **Did you know?** Small businesses may experience numerous ransomware attempts EVERY day! Sonicwall The Year of Ransomware Report 2021

A firewall is a security system that monitors and controls incoming and outgoing network traffic based on predetermined security rules and policies. The name, firewall, is borrowed from a building architectural feature constructed to prevent the spread of fires: "a firewall is a fire-resistant barrier used to prevent the spread of fire". Firewalls are built between or through buildings, structures, or electrical substation transformers, or within an aircraft or vehicle.

A computer firewall separates your local network from the

outside world, so you can print and share files locally, and you don't get unwanted visitors. Firewalls are typically deployed to prevent unauthorized access to or from a private network. They can be hardware-based or software-based. Firewalls can prevent unauthorized access to a network, protect against malware and other types of malicious activity, and help enforce compliance with security policies. Additionally, firewalls can be used to monitor and log network traffic, a useful feature for detecting and investigating security incidents.

Business-class firewalls provide better protection through additional security features and enhanced reporting capabilities. As an example, legacy firewalls and other traditional security controls lack the capability or processing power to detect, inspect, and mitigate threats sent over HTTPS traffic.

Many of us have been taught to look for the "s" so we're confident we're dealing with a secure network. Criminals know this and can easily apply a certificate to their site to trick you. It "looks" more legit, but it's not. Many basic firewalls can't inspect traffic that's encrypted, and you need a more sophisticated firewall that can do "deep packet inspection" to identify and stop the threats the criminals are trying to hide. This is why we typically recommend a "Business Class" firewall for a business.

$$\triangle\triangle\triangle$$

Firewall:

Protect Yourself On-Line – Cyber Fit Next Steps and Things to Know

✓   Invest in a business class firewall if you run a business. The basic protections provided by your Internet Service Provider aren't enough in this day and age.

DAY #18 – WI-FI SAFETY

THE LATEST ENVIRONMENTAL CRISIS: WIRELESS DATA POLLUTION.

© Glasbergen/ glasbergen.com

>> **Wi-Fi** is a technology that allows electronic devices to connect to a local network without physical cables.

>> **Did you know?** In the US, 47% of people say they use public Wi-Fi regularly – High Speed Internet Survey

Before 1997, to get your computer onto a network so you could access printers, servers, Internet gateways, and other network services, you took a cable and physically plugged it into your computer and a network switch. The invention of wifi (originally created by the 802.11 committee) created standards by which computers and devices could use radio transceivers to wirelessly connect to networks. Along with this convenience, it became possible for bad actors to break into your network without even entering your building. A hacker can drive by your building, get in range of your wifi signals without leaving their car, and perform their mischief without you ever physically detecting their presence. Secure wifi protocols are essential for protecting your business from such attacks.

The first step is to keep your technology up to date. If you have a very old wireless access point, you probably don't have access to the current encryption standards (or network speed!). The old encryption standard was WEP, and the current standard is WPA2 or better. The older standards mean it would be easier for someone to break into your network. Other important steps include:

-    Name your network something that doesn't directly show that its yours. The SSID stands for Service Set Identifier, and it's your network's name. You can call your network anything you like.
-    The password also should be a STRONG password, to make it harder for any unwelcome guests to get on your network. Never use the default password that comes with the device. These are very easy to look up! Note that without a strong password, someone could sit in your parking lot and connect to your network without your knowledge. The could even log into and reprogram your firewall.
-    All technology has vulnerabilities, so just like the rest of your tech, keep your firewalls up to date with the latest security updates from your vendor – "firmware updates".
-    If other non-employees are going to use your network, set up a "guest" network. You can share a single Internet connection so it doesn't cost more, but this way, guests can connect to the Internet without getting on your main network.

When you are not at work, finding a strong Wi-Fi signal for your phone or laptop can feel like an exciting victory, a sanctuary - no need to consume your data plan and you get a stronger signal - but it can come with risks. Public Wi-Fi is risky because it is typically unsecured and unencrypted. This means that anyone on the same network can potentially see and intercept the data being sent and received by other users. For example, if you're connected to a public Wi-Fi network and you're entering sensitive information such as login credentials, credit card information, or personal data, a hacker could potentially intercept and steal that information. Additionally, unsecured networks can also be used to spread malware and other malicious software.

Another risk is the possibility of using a rogue access point, which is a wireless access point that has been set up by a hacker to mimic a legitimate network. Once connected to a rogue access point, a hacker can intercept and redirect your internet traffic to a malicious website, steal your data, or infect your device with malware.

Lastly, Public Wi-Fi networks are not always secure, and hackers can easily use tools to hack into a public Wi-Fi network and gain access to all the connected devices, steal personal information, and monitor internet activities. It is recommended to use a virtual private network (VPN) to encrypt your internet connection when using public Wi-Fi. Also, be careful about what you do online when connected to a public network, and turn off automatic connections so you don't inadvertently connect to an unsecured network. If your smart phone wireless data connection is strong and your data plan sufficient, it is always safer to directly connect to your wireless phone carrier through a personal hotspot on your phone than to connect through a public wireless network.

△△△

Wi-Fi:

Protect Yourself On-Line – Cyber Fit Next Steps and Things to Know

- ✓ Change your default Wi-Fi router password.
- ✓ Enable WPA-2 or higher encryption.

✓   Make sure your local router firmware is up to date.

✓   If you have smart devices (IoT), make sure they have updated firmware.

✓   Use your mobile phone's personal hotspot in lieu of a public wireless network whenever feasible.

DAY #19 - POLICIES AND PROCEDURES

© Glasbergen/ glasbergen.com

"The boss is worried about information security, so he sends his messages one alphabet letter at a time in random sequence.'

>> Cybersecurity **policies and procedures** provide a framework for how employees should use technology and handle sensitive information. They establish guidelines and best practices for maintaining a secure and compliant IT environment.

>> **Did you know?** Nearly half (45%) of employees admit to opening emails they consider to be suspicious and the same percentage admit they don't report suspicious emails to their IT or security teams. (2020 Survey by Internet security company Mimecast, reported in Dark Reading).

Computer Acceptable Use Policies and Procedures are important because they help to protect an organization's assets (including its networks, computers, software, and data) from unauthorized access, use, disclosure, disruption, modification, or destruction. If you run a local business, you want to be sure everyone understands the rules. If you work at a business, you'll want to be a good company citizen and follow the rules to help ensure safely. You should also consider creating a simple policy to get your family talking and on the same page.

Policies and procedures help to ensure that an organization's computer resources are used in an efficient and ethical manner, and that they are not used for illegal or malicious activities. Additionally, these policies and procedures help to protect the organization from legal liability and reputational damage. Overall, computer acceptable use policies and procedures play a critical role in maintaining the security and integrity of an organization's computer systems and resources.

Acceptable use policy spells out in detail exactly what is allowed and what is not allowed on a company (or home) network. Are your children allowed to use your computer?

Here are a few questions to think about when forming your policies, either for home or in the office:

- **Security:** Users should be made aware of the importance of keeping their login credentials secure and not sharing them with others. If for example, a password needs to be shared, how should it be securely shared?
- **Internet usage:** Specify what types of websites and online activities are permitted and prohibited while on the company's network. Can someone go to any website they want? What is considered inappropriate? Can employees surf personal websites during breaks?
- **Email usage:** Specify how email should be used and what types of messages are acceptable.
- **File sharing:** Specify how files should be shared and

what types of files are acceptable to share. If an employee is planning to work from home, is it ok to put files on a service like DropBox to access later?

- **Personal use:** Specify what types of personal use of company-owned computers and networks are permitted, if any. Can you connect your personal phone to the company WIFI to get a better connection or save on data usage? Can family members use a work laptop if its not currently in use at home?

- **Privacy:** Specify how the company will protect the privacy of users and the data stored on company-owned computers and networks. Can employers review employee emails or browsing history? What privacy considerations should be expected?

- **Compliance:** Specify that users must comply with all relevant laws and regulations. Industry regulations, and state requirements could include hefty fines for breaking rules – are you current on all the requirements?

- **Consequences:** Specify the consequences for failing to comply with the policy, such as disciplinary action or termination of employment.

Get people talking and work to reach common ground on how computers should be used. The star employee who's doing extra work after hours may wind up infecting your network with a virus they brought in from home. What will you do about that?

It is important to note that the policy should be reviewed and updated regularly to reflect any changes in technology, laws, and the company's needs.

What cyber security policies are being used in your office?

- ☐ Acceptable Use Policy
- ☐ Password Policy
- ☐ Data Confidentiality Policy
- ☐ Mobile Device Policy
- ☐ Bring Your Own Device (BYOD) Policy

☐ Incident Response Policy
☐ Backup and Disaster Recovery Plan
☐ Business Continuity Plan
☐ Remote Access Policy
☐ IT Asset Disposal Policy
☐ Security Awareness Policy
☐ 3rd-Party Access Policy
☐ Removable Media Policy (USB Drives/Sticks)
☐ User Termination Policy

Do employees sign off that they have read and understand these policies?

If you're an employee, remember that cybersecurity is a team sport and everyone's roles matter. The purpose of policies and procedures isn't to create more busy work for you – it's about keeping your company, your customers, and you more secure.

ΔΔΔ

Policies and Procedures:

Protect Yourself On-Line – Cyber Fit Next Steps and Things to Know

✓ Create some basic technology policies and procedures for your team – your business or your home. Policies should balance the need to effectively use technology AND keep everyone safe.

✓ Understand and discuss the "WHY" behind each rule.

DAY #20 - PHYSICAL SECURITY

"I tried computer dating, but my computer
says it wants to be just friends."

>> **Physical security** is an important part of a comprehensive cybersecurity program because it helps protect the physical assets and infrastructure that support a business's technology systems and data. Without proper physical security measures in place, cybercriminals could potentially gain access to a business's physical assets, such as servers, network equipment, and storage devices. With physical access, they can gain unauthorized access to sensitive data or disrupt the business's operations.

>> **Did you know?** 57% of employees have scribbled work related passwords on sticky notes – Survey by Keeper Security.

There are a lot of ways hackers will use technology to disrupt your data, but don't forget physical security of your home and office. Here's a list of deterrents:

- **Lock Screens** – When you step away from your computer, lock the screen. You can set a timer to autolock upon a timeout after keyboard inactivity (type lock screen settings into your Windows Search on the lower left of your computer screen), or just get in the habit of hitting the Windows Key followed by the "L" key. That's a great keyboard shortcut to remember.
- Consider a **physical lock** on a laptop in a high traffic area.
- Practice a **clean desk policy**. Don't leave any sensitive documents on your desk.
- **No passwords on post-its!** Not on your monitor, not under your keyboard… don't do it!
- **Lock your file cabinet**. Restrict physical access to any protected information.
- If you keep a server onsite, **lock your server** in a data room.
- Encrypt your laptop. Laptops are small, valuable, and easy to grab, and easy to hide. A stolen laptop can easily receive up to 50% of its value in cash, so they are attractive targets. Physically protect your laptop – don't leave it exposed in a car, or on the counter of a coffee shop. But if it is stolen, encryption can keep the criminals away from your data.
- Consider using **mobile device management** to be able to wipe data off a lost or stolen laptop, phone, or tablet.
- Consider applying a **screen protector** to your device to hide your screen from wandering eyes. These are very inexpensive, attach right onto your screen, and restrict the viewing angle of the screen to prevent your airplane seat or coffee shop table neighbor from taking a gander.

Cyber threats aren't the only risks to be mindful of. Physical security also plays a role in keeping sensitive information protected. How often do employees mistakenly leave a mobile device or computer unattended or left behind in a taxi or restaurant.   It can happen to anyone. But, if someone were to swipe an unattended phone or log in to sensitive assets from a connected network session, all your data could immediately be at risk.

This is an area of security often overlooked and in need of a good refresher, especially with so many employees now accustomed to working from home and out of practice complying with good office security measures.

Properly discarding information.   When throwing away documents, users should be sure not to place sensitive papers into a general trash bin. The company should have a policy and process in place for appropriate and secure removal of paperwork. Use a shredder, or if you have a lot of paper, get a shredding service.

Electronics recycling and hard drive shredding:

Did you know that computers, monitors, and other electronic devices can't be thrown away in regular trash?   These items require special treatment by authorized electronics recycling providers to ensure environmental safety. Benefit of of electronic recycling include:

-       Keeping harmful chemicals out of landfills.   Did you know that computers contain a lot of harmful chemicals like chromium, beryllium, cadmium, mercury, and bromine.
-       Re-use of salvaged parts and components to decrease the need for new consumption.

Hard drive shredding is an essential practice to ensure the protection of data that may reside on equipment your are throwing away. Benefits include:

- Peace of Mind - if you really want to be sure your data can't be retrieved later, shredding ensures total destruction. Proper handling of protected information is an important part of any cybersecurity plan.

- Compliance - Regulations like HIPAA require the protection of sensitive information.
- DeClutter - The "paperless" office was supposed to streamline the world, but we just end up with more digital and physical clutter as time goes by - clear it out and de-stress!

In 2022, Morgan Stanley was fined $35 million to settle allegations that it failed to ensure the proper disposal of hard drives containing personally identifiable information for 15 million customers. Don't let your own data wind up in a dumpster or at an auction. Shred your old data! In addition to the financial penalty, the firm was also required to "adopt written policies and procedures that address administrative, technical, and physical safeguards for the protection of customer records and information."

△△△

Physical Security:

Protect Yourself On-Line – Cyber Fit Next Steps and Things to Know

- ✓ Invest in the right equipment that lasts longer.
- ✓ Repair what you can to keep equipment longer.
- ✓ When possible - re-purpose functioning equipment.
- ✓ Use authorized electronics recycling providers to dispose of end-of-life equipment. Help educate others - no electronics in the trash!
- ✓ Shred hard disks and get destruction certificates for especially sensitive data.

DAY #21 – CYBERSECURITY EDUCATION - KEEP LEARNING!

© Glasbergen/ glasbergen.com

"Yesterday I changed everyone's password to 'password'.
I sent it to everyone in a memo, put it on a big sign on the wall
and printed it on all of the coffee cups. Guess how many people
called me this morning because they forgot the password."

>>**Cybersecurity Awareness Training** is designed to educate individuals and employees about best practices for protecting sensitive information and data from cyber threats.

>> **Did you know?** 32% of untrained end users will fail a simulated phishing test – KnowBe4's 2022 Phishing by Industry Benchmarking Report.

Cybersecurity is not a "set it and forget it" topic. As we depend more and more on technology, cybersecurity is increasingly playing a fundamental role in all our lives. In this day and age, we're all techies – we're on our smart phones and laptops keeping in touch with friends, ordering take out, catching up on email, paying our bills, setting our thermostats remotely, you name it! "I'm not a techie" doesn't work anymore – cybersecurity is everyone's responsibility.

As consumers demand more information about how their data is protected, companies are building up their cybersecurity reputations. Recently Walmart hosted its first cyber media day, and they're starting to focus on consumer cybersecurity education with tips on their website. In Finland, researchers at Aalto University are developing an education package for all European Union member states, with digital literacy being recognized as a civic skill. We'll see more efforts like this worldwide, and my motivation for putting together this book is to be part of the cybersecurity education movement.

De-Mystifying Cybersecurity

As you've seen, there's no "silver bullet" when it comes to cybersecurity, and technology solutions can only go so far. Learn as much as you can and remember that cybersecurity requires your participation – it's EVERYONE'S responsibility. The Massachusetts Data Security Law (and similar regulations around the country), as well as other industry-specific regulations like HIPAA and CMMC, all *specifically require* ongoing cybersecurity education for a reason.

Cybersecurity is a bit of a "cat and mouse game" with criminals constantly working on new and devious ways to cash in. By reading this book, you're well on your way to being more cyber secure, but cybersecurity is a topic that keeps requiring attention. It requires your continuing to stay up to date on the news. Keep your best practices going forward and develop a *culture* of cybersecurity with the people around you, whether it's your family, your community, or your business.

I never thought it would happen to me.

Keep an eye on the news and get familiar with the latest threats. I have said it many times throughout this book and here it is again: think before you click! In our local community, we've seen very bright people fall for tricks – the fake Microsoft pop-up that says there's a problem on your computer and to call the hotline right away, or the fake invoice or password reset request in your inbox. When we run simulated phishing tests as part of training exercises for the local businesses we work with, there is almost always someone who clicks on the link. Had it been a real threat, that person would have effectively opened the door to the criminal. The more you know about what the criminals are attempting, the safer you'll be online. Tax season scams, gift card scams, password reset scams – get familiar with these, and talk to your family members about this. Remember the Nigerian Prince Scam? Often the subject of jokes, it's eye-opening to note that American's lost $700,000 to these types of scams in 2019, according to a report by ADT Security Services.

Stay ahead of cyber threats: Learn from the latest news headlines.

Be brave and keep up with the news, going beyond just the headline. Don't let the news scare you into thinking it's all gloom and doom, and don't let the news trick you into a false sense of security that only the big businesses that make the headlines like Marriott, Colonial Pipeline, or Yahoo need to worry. It's not about what your data is worth to someone else, it's about what it's worth to YOU. As we've shown in this book, most threats today are automated and indiscriminate. How would it feel if you lost your family's lifetime of family photos? Have you talked to your local service providers about how they protect your data? Have you talked to your family about cybersecurity?

Everyone can help!

Cybersecurity is no longer just an issue for IT departments, but rather one that impacts everyone - at home, at work, and in our daily lives. A cyberattack or data breach can result in significant financial loss, identity theft, or damage to a business's reputation, all of which can have a lasting impact on individuals and families. From personal devices to online accounts and financial information, we are all vulnerable to cyber threats, and need to take steps to protect ourselves and our assets. By being aware of potential threats, adopting strong security practices, and staying informed about the latest threats and trends, we can better safeguard our personal and professional lives, and help ensure a safer and more secure digital future.

There's no such thing as 100% security, but the more layers of protection you have, the safer you are against data loss, breaches, and downtime. The cyber threat level has increased dramatically over the past few years, and to even maintain the same level of risk, you'll need to increase security. Let's shift the conversation towards how everyone can contribute to the collective security effort.

We're all in this together.

Cybersecurity is a collective effort, and the contributions of *everyone* involved can make a significant difference. By increasing your knowledge of cybersecurity, you can better protect yourself online, and adopt a "cyberfit" mindset that prioritizes continuous learning and improvement to help you stay ahead of evolving threats.

Cybersecurity requires your participation!

△△△

Cybersecurity Education – Keep Learning:

Protect Yourself On-Line – Cyber Fit Next Steps and Things to Know

- ✓ Put cyber anxiety aside and read the news – stay up to date with the headlines and trends by reading at least one article a week.
- ✓ Recognize that most threats are not targeted but are rather indiscriminate – *anyone* can be affected.
- ✓ Participate – Take action. Cybersecurity is not a spectator

sport.
- ✓ Talk to your family, business, community – EVERYONE can help!
- ✓ Create a culture of Cybersecurity Awareness at home and at work.

CONGRATULATIONS!
HERE'S YOUR 21 DAY CYBER FIT RE-CAP:

1. Keep your Tech up-to-date

✓ Have you been postponing updates? Say "yes" today to your systems' security update prompts! The updates are free!

✓ Take action to replace any active hardware older than 5 years.

✓ Upgrade or dispose of any tech that is no longer supported – do not keep past end-of-life.

✓ Protect your security and protect the environment when you dispose of old hardware. (More about the data security aspects on Day 20)

2. Strong Passwords

✓ Did you recognize any of your passwords on the most popular passwords list? Put the book down and change any of those passwords RIGHT NOW!

✓ Use STRONG passwords: A combination of uppercase and lowercase letters, numbers, and symbols at least 12 characters long.

✓ Don't re-use passwords across different sites or recycled for the same site.

✓ Change password when a breach occurs – (and this is why you don't use a PW across multiple sites). If one of companies you do business with like Target, or Chase Bank gets breached, change your password. Keep up with the news headlines.

✓ Don't overshare on social media – criminals can use this information to potentially access our accounts.

3. Use a Password Manager

✓ Use a password manager to facilitate good password hygiene (strong, unique passwords).

✓ Be aware of the limitations of a password manager – there is a risk, but the risk of weak passwords is greater. Use a VERY STRONG vault password (with Multi Factor Authentication which we'll review in the next chapter).

✓ Be aware that through no fault of your own, third-party breaches may occur, and you will need to change those passwords.

✓ Don't store passwords in browsers. If you have passwords saved in browsers, change the password and DO NOT save it to the browser again.

4. Multi Factor Authentication

✓ Have you skipped any requests to set up MFA? Set it up now on all your accounts!

✓ When possible, create an alternate verification process (e.g. an email address or voice call) in case you lose your mobile phone.

✓ Yes, MFA is inconvenient – do it anyway!

5. Inventory

✓ Take an inventory of all hardware, software, online services you use. Identify and define your assets: Determine what your critical assets are, including data, applications, systems, and endpoints. Important data may wind up where you don't expect it. Scanners, for example, can retain information on hard drives.

✓ Use software tools to search your local area network – you may find things you don't even know about.

✓ Establish protocols around shadow IT.

6. Phishing

✓ <u>Never</u> use the same password for multiple sites.

✓ Track the breaches you're involved with (for example your bank, or any online application you use) to know when your info is leaked.

✓ Don't assume an email containing personal information about you must be legitimate. As we've seen before, this could be from the Dark Web (previous breaches) or harvested from social media.

✓ Phishing emails may be very difficult to spot, so stay alert. Years ago, they would contain poor graphics and bad grammar. Not anymore.

✓ Don't overreact to emails with threatening information. More than likely they are just part of a bulk anonymous email campaign.

✓ Watch for "seasonal" phishing campaigns such as tax refunds in the Spring, shopping around the holidays, and election info during election season.

✓ If an email is unexpected, pause before clicking.

✓ Don't follow the links or phone numbers in suspicious emails. Call the number on the back of a credit card or go directly to the web site in question for follow up.

✓ Use an email security filter to help reduce scam emails. However, remember that no spam filter is 100%. Cyber criminals work hard to get the threat through.

7. Domain Registration

✓ If you own a domain name, protect it by ensuring your information is kept up to date for renewals, and you protect the account with MFA.

✓ Watch out so you don't get tricked by similar domain names – a common technique used by criminals is to register a similar sounding domain name to one of your favorites – check the spelling carefully. Also watch for an alternative ".net" or foreign domains like .ru or .cn when you're not expecting them.

8. Email Security

✓ 90% of cyber threats enter through email – Think about that every time you open your email.

✓ Keep your inbox de-cluttered with an email security filter - A cluttered inbox leads to mistakes.

✓ SLOW DOWN. Think before you click! Criminals don't need a backdoor if they can enter through the front door – Your email inbox.

9. Zero Trust

✓ Make effective use of passwords and MFA – They always matter!

✓ Identify and define your assets: Determine what your critical assets are, including data, applications, systems, and endpoints.

✓ Segment your network: Divide your network into smaller, segmented sections to limit the impact of a potential security breach.

✓ Implement least privilege: Limit the access of users and devices to only the resources and systems they need to perform their job.

10. Know your Regulations

✓ Get acquainted with the relevant regulations that apply to both you and your business.

✓ Learn from these requirements – they're designed to help you stay more secure. They exist for a reason: to help improve security.

✓ Tackle one regulation at a time – don't get overwhelmed.

11. Cyber Insurance

✓ If you're running a local business, get cyber insurance to help protect you financially in the event of an incident. Individual insurance coverage is also becoming available.

✓ Be vigilant in managing and enhance your security

practices. Insurance is NOT a replacement for good cyber controls. An insurance policy won't prevent an incident.
✓ Be prepared to handle downtime, reputation damage, and stress – these are not within the scope of cyber insurance.
✓   Review your policy to understand what's covered and what's not covered, especially sub-limits for different types of requests.

12. Cyber Resilience

✓   Expect to have to confront a cyber incident. It's not a matter of IF, but rather WHEN it will happen.
✓ Have a Plan
✓ Revisit the Plan
✓ Report the Crime

13. IoT – Internet of Things

✓   Keep an inventory of EVERYTHING you own that's connected to the Internet. Take a walk around your home and office; you may be surprised how many connected devices you find.
✓ Change default passwords.
✓ Update firmware when available.
✓ Use a separate guest network for IoT devices.

14. Backups

✓ Identify your most important data.
✓ Decide how much data you can tolerate losing.
✓ Decide how much downtime you can tolerate.
✓ Set up an appropriate backup that covers your needs.
✓ TEST your backup by trying to recover a file.

15. Encryption

✓ Never email protected information – it's the equivalent of sending very private information on a postcard.
✓   The "S" in HTTS:// means traffic to a website is encrypted, but with low cost and free security certificates widely available, know that it doesn't mean the site is safe

(criminals love this trick!).

16. Antivirus and Endpoint Protection

✓ Confirm you are running antivirus software. Microsoft Windows Defender is a good basic antivirus tool.

✓ Confirm your antivirus software is active and up-to-date. Commercial antivirus products run on a subscription model and need to be renewed.

✓ Consider Endpoint Detection and Response (EDR) software if you deem your environment requires more advanced and better protection.

17. Firewall

✓ Invest in a business class firewall if you run a business. The basic protections provided by your Internet Service Provider aren't enough in this day and age.

18. WIFI

✓ Change your default Wi-Fi router password.

✓ Enable WPA-2 or higher encryption.

✓ Make sure your local router firmware is up to date.

✓ If you have smart devices (IoT), make sure they have updated firmware.

✓ Use your mobile phone's personal hotspot in lieu of a public wireless network whenever feasible.

19. Policies and Procedures

✓ Create some basic technology policies and procedures for your team – your business or your home. Policies should balance the need to effectively use technology AND keep everyone safe.

✓ Understand and discuss the "WHY" behind each rule.

20. Physical Security

✓ Invest in the right equipment that lasts longer.

✓ Repair what you can to keep equipment longer.

✓ When possible - re-purpose functioning equipment.

✓ Use authorized electronics recycling providers to

dispose of end-of-life equipment. Help educate others - no electronics in the trash!

✓ Shred hard disks and get destruction certificates for especially sensitive data.

21. Cyber Education – Keep Learning!

✓ Put cyber anxiety aside and read the news – stay up to date with the headlines and trends by reading at least one article a week.

✓ Recognize that most threats are not targeted but are rather indiscriminate – *anyone* can be affected.

✓ Participate – Take action. Cybersecurity is not a spectator sport.

✓ Talk to your family, business, community – EVERYONE can help!

✓ Create a culture of Cybersecurity Awareness at home and at work.

APPENDIX – RESOURCES

©Glasbergen
glasbergen.com

"My term paper is almost finished. I updated my software, defragmented my hard drive, bookmarked an online dictionary, and installed new ink cartridges. Now all I need are some words and a topic!"

- **Internet Crime Complaint Center (IC3)** <Part of the FBI> https://www.ic3.gov/Home/ComplaintChoice/default.aspx
- **National Cyber Security Alliance (NCSA)**: www.Staysafeonline.org
- **National Institute of Standards and Technology (NIST) "Cybersecurity is Everyone's Job" guidebook:** https://www.nist.gov/news- events/news/2018/10/cybersecurity-everyones-job
- **NIST Small Business Cybersecurity Corner**: https://www.nist.gov/itl/smallbusinesscyber
- **Federal Trade Commission (FTC) small business resources**: www.ftc.gov/smb
- **Center for Internet Security (CIS) Controls for SME**: https://

www.cisecurity.org/white-papers/cis-controls-sme-guide/

- **Technology News Sites**: www.computerworld.com, www.bleepingcomputer.com, www.zdnet.com, https://www.cnn.com/business/tech, https://www.foxnews.com/tech

- **Federal Bureau of Investigation**: www.fbi.gov/investigate/cyber

- **Department of Homeland Security:** www.dhs.gov/topic/cybersecurity

- **Cybersecurity & Infrastructure Security Agency (CISA)**: https://www.cisa.gov/

- **MITRE ATT&CK®** is a globally-accessible knowledge base of adversary tactics and techniques based on real-world observations. https://attack.mitre.org/

ABOUT THE AUTHOR

Ann Westerheim, Ph. D.

Ann Westerheim, PhD is the Founder and President of Ekaru, a Technology Service Provider of cybersecurity and IT services for small and medium businesses in the greater Boston area. Ann is an accomplished technology innovator and leader with three engineering degrees from MIT. She has over twenty years of high tech experience in  research, advanced development, product development, and as an entrepreneur. Her career has spanned a vast range of technology endeavors including research in thin film semiconductors and superconductors, microprocessor fabrication, development of early Internet medical applications, and now focusing on the application of technology in business. She holds two patents and has an avid focus on the "last mile" of technology and decreasing the digital divide.

Connect with me on LinkedIn:
https://www.linkedin.com/in/annwesterheim/